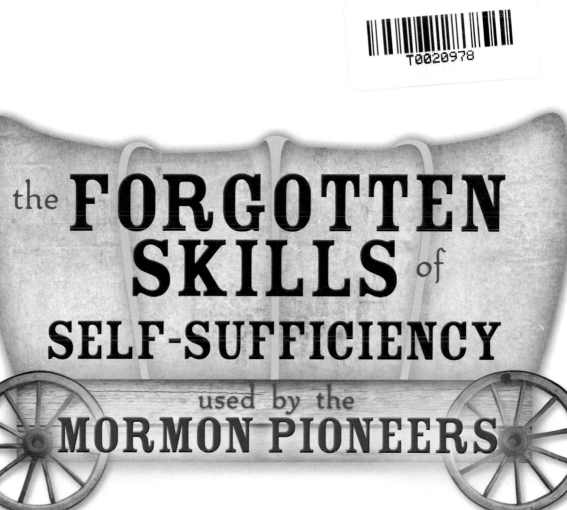

the FORGOTTEN SKILLS of
SELF-SUFFICIENCY
used by the
MORMON PIONEERS

CALEB WARNOCK

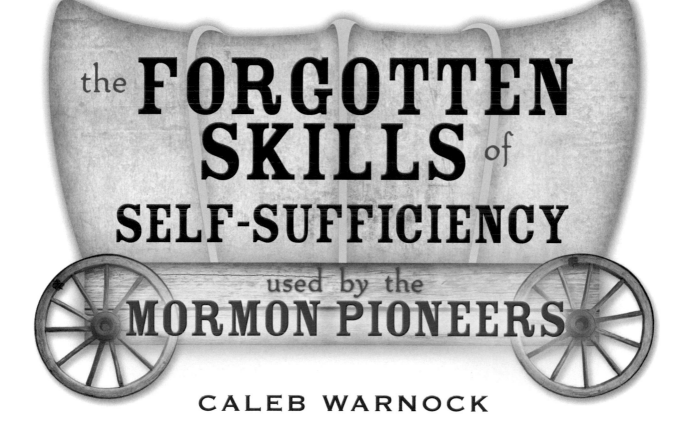

the FORGOTTEN SKILLS of SELF-SUFFICIENCY used by the MORMON PIONEERS

CALEB WARNOCK

BONNEVILLE BOOKS
SPRINGVILLE, UTAH

The views expressed within this work are the sole responsibility of the author and do not necessarily reflect the position of Cedar Fort, Inc., or any other entity.

ISBN 13: 978-1-59955-510-2

LIBRARY OF CONGRESS CATALOGING-IN-PUBLICATION DATA

Warnock, Caleb (Caleb J.), 1973- author.
  The forgotten skills of self-sufficiency used by the Mormon pioneers /
Caleb Warnock.
     pages cm
  Includes bibliographical references.
  ISBN 978-1-59955-510-2
  1. Self-reliant living--Handbooks, manuals, etc. 2. Mormon
pioneers--Social life and customs. I. Title.

 GF78.W37 2011
 640--dc22

                          2010046688

Published by Bonneville Books, an imprint of Cedar Fort, Inc.,
2373 W. 700 S., Springville, UT 84663
Distributed by Cedar Fort, Inc., www.cedarfort.com

Cover and page design by Danie Romrell
Cover design © 2011 by Lyle Mortimer
Edited by Melissa J. Caldwell

Printed in the United States of America

10 9 8 7

Printed on acid-free paper

For my grandparents and parents who taught me to think, then work:
Phill & "Billie" Nielson, Robert & Phyllis Warnock, DeWayne & Pat Warnock

CONTENTS

SPECIAL THANKS

To the "Buy the Book" writers group for years of truth and "buckets of love":
Laura Andersen, Ginger Churchill, Matt and Brooklyn Evans, Jenifer Lee,
Eric James Stone

To the "Smashing Stories" writers group for investing time in talent:
Maegan Langer, Steph Lineback, Scott Livingston, Janiel Miller,
Cally Stephens-Nielson, Loraine Scott, Maleah Warner

To the American Fork Arts Council,
and particularly Lori England, for their support of local writers,
to all my students over the years,
to the team at Cedar Fort Publishing for believing in this book,
to the fantastic staff of the Orem Public Library and Utah's Pioneer Online Library,
and to Barbara Christiansen for her early reading of the manuscript.

Most of all, to the beauty who transplanted raspberries on our first date,
my wife, Charmayne. You are the poetry of my life. This book is for you.

PREFACE

I have just come in from gathering the last eggs of the day, a half dozen in shades of brown, white, and green. Triple-digit heat scorched us today, and now the rolling night air is a pleasure and relief. As I write, platinum lightning splits the night sky over central Utah, accompanied by the primordial crack of thunder.

Blasting thunder and strobe lightning are among the last physical connections today's gardeners have to the pioneers who settled this land. The sound, especially in July, still forebodes either a welcome cloudburst or the threat of wildfire along the sun-dried mountainside, and sometimes both. Usually, summer dusk provides a pause for a last check of the garden crops, a moment to list the tasks of the upcoming day. But not tonight. Tonight, I've been chased indoors by Mother Nature.

Most gardens in the West have just begun to yield in July. August brings an unparalleled bounty

Purple Dame's Rocket flowers in bloom in spring beneath apple trees. The family barn can be glimpsed through the trees.

from the soil, followed by September's grand finale of winter squash, grapes, pumpkins for carving, and the last beans from the vines.

But this narrowed window of plenty is a modern invention.

For millennia, families could have ill afforded to harvest sustenance from the garden only three months of the year. A year-round supply of homegrown foodstuffs was the only insurance against starvation. Using truly simple techniques, homestead families harvested sweet, crisp carrots out of the snow-blanketed garden soil in December, January, and February. Still today, those who have tasted winter carrots recall longingly their sugary flavor and snappy texture, outweighing by far carrots harvested at any other time of the year. These days, fresh winter garden carrots are among the rarest of vegetables.

The pioneers raised robust summer vegetables without expensive seed catalogs or nurseries. They created spectacular flower gardens at no cost. They ate fresh out of the garden twelve months a year, a skill that has now all but vanished. Their self-sufficiency provided security against lost wages, harsh weather, economic depression and recession, and commercial contamination and shortages.

Until World War II, the backyard harvest was almost the inverse of today's garden. The harvest extended so far across the calendar that a simple phrase described the brief time when the garden could not be counted on to feed the family. In lean years, that "hunger gap" lasted from late winter, when the stored food and winter vegetables had been used up, until the first perennial greens appeared in spring. Few now recall that when the pilgrims arrived at Plymouth Rock, dandelions did not dot the United States. The plants were brought here later by immigrants who valued them for being the plant that broke the hunger gap each spring, for both people and honeybees.

Today, that pioneer ability to provide food security and self-reliance has never been more appealing to families. As food and fuel prices fluctuate, many of us are taking a deeper look at homegrown food, thrift, and self-sufficient living. In a sign of our uncertain economic times, families across the country are even beginning to keep chickens again. There is a growing desire to learn anew the skills of independence that marked the lives of the Mormon pioneers.

Many of their techniques are now lost to the general population. I was lucky enough to grow up in the kitchens and gardens of the last generation to provide family meals without relying on the grocery store. My great-grandmother's "supermarket" was her garden and storeroom. My grandparents shook their heads at bland, store-bought vegetables. They managed their family budgets by putting to work centuries of received wisdom about food and self-reliant living. This book attempts to record some of what remains known of their methods, to demonstrate just how simple and fulfilling the path to increased providence can be—along with the pleasure of eating fresh garden produce with robust, homegrown flavor all year round.

This is not a book about bottling peaches or digging a root cellar. This book begins to overcome the myth that self-reliant living is practical only for up-before-dawn farmers or green-thumb gardeners with huge yards and no social life. The reality is that self-sufficiency need not be elaborate, time-consuming, or backbreaking. Any modern family can be strengthened by discovering the forgotten skills of self-sufficient living used by the Mormon pioneers.

The sweet smell of moisture perfumes the air now. Outside the open window of my home office, the first rain in weeks has just begun to fall.

—Caleb Warnock, Utah County, Utah
Tuesday, July 20, 2010
9:32 p.m.

Raspberries, cabbages, potatoes and peas in early spring can be seen in the background, with yucca and rhubarb in the foreground.

Cabbages in spring have reached full-head size just as broccoli is beginning to produce florets. The earliest zucchini of the year can be seen in bloom behind the onions.

CHAPTER 1

THE SELF-PROVIDENT HOME GARDEN

The first fruit of the garden is family. Then knowledge. Then vegetables.

In a literal and even surprising way, self-sufficient gardening is rooted in understanding our link to the ancestors who came before us. Turning the hearts of the children to the fathers has a direct impact on the family garden that is rarely talked about anymore.

Both the food we eat today and the food the pioneers grew in their day are direct gifts from those who came before. Take corn, for example. Scientists now believe they have identified, in Mexico, the original ancestor of modern corn. The plant resembles a wild grass with a few kernels of corn on tufts. First Native Americans and then homesteaders spent lifetimes breeding this plant to create what we now know as modern corn.

The vegetables and fruits we eat today are the result of the careful and fastidious selection of traits over centuries. Originally purple and yellow, the orange carrots are another example of how our food was born out of the intelligent labor of our ancestors. All told, the labor, time, and creative effort required to breed the vegetables, fruits, and even meat protein—cows, chickens, turkeys—that we enjoy today is the literal fruit of generations.

Quietly, and almost unnoticed, the majority of this work has now been lost.

Multi-colored carrots from the author's garden. Wild carrots, which grow rampant in Utah as the weed "Queen Anne's Lace," are white. All other colors have been cultivated over centuries. Purple and yellow carrots were common varieties centuries ago. Orange carrots are historically recent.

- Almost 96 percent of the commercial vegetable varieties available in 1903 are now extinct, according to the American Museum of Natural History's Center for Biodiversity and Conservation.[1]

- Eight of the fifteen breeds of pigs raised in the United States fifty years ago are now extinct, along with sixty breeds of chickens that were raised in the United States prior to World War II, according to the American Livestock Breeds Conservancy.[2]

These breeds, both vegetable and animal, have died out for two reasons: first, fewer breeds were needed because of the industrialization of food. Those favored breeds focused on fast, uniform production of vegetables and meat that would ship well not only across the country but around the world. Second, as grocery stores became more available, fewer families needed to spend the time required to raise their own vegetables and protein. Even fewer worked to continue pure breeding lines, both in animals and vegetables.

Notes

1. Center for Biodiversity and Conservation, "Biodiversity and Your Food."
2. American Livestock Breeds Conservancy, "Rare Breed Facts."

CHAPTER 2

A MODERN RETURN TO PIONEER SEED-SAVING

Pioneer Lorenzo Dow Young, the youngest brother of Brigham Young, entered Salt Lake Valley on July 24, 1847, having "made the trip with one two-horse team one four-ox team and also brought a cow and some chickens. His first act after arriving in the valley was to plant a few potatoes that he had brought with him from the frontier. He succeeded in raising and saving a few small tubers for seed. The next year he raised a few more which he dealt out in two quart lots to some of his fellow settlers."

—"Lorenzo Dow Young" *History of Utah: Biographical*

Grow a hybrid seed, eat for a summer. Grow an open-pollinated seed, eat for generations.

Any family can increase their preparedness by understanding the benefits of traditional, open-pollinated seed. As the pioneers crossed the plains, among their prized possessions was garden seed and grain for planting—their food security. On July 22, 1847, an advance party of Saints entered Salt Lake Valley to plant potatoes, turnips, beans, and buckwheat. On that day, the garden season was half-gone, but the pioneers knew exactly which rapid-growing crops could yield food by autumn and produce critical seed.

Learn from the Pioneers

"The pioneers planted potatoes immediately. Some of them began planting even before they had their first meal in the valley. The ground was so hard that some of their plows broke, so they built a dam in a creek to flood the ground and soften it. Then they dug ditches to bring water from the mountain streams to the crops. This was one of the earliest uses of modern irrigation methods. Trappers and mountain men such as Jim Bridger had said that crops would never grow in the Salt Lake Valley, but by irrigating the land, the pioneers were able to successfully produce crops. . . . The pioneers continued to irrigate more land and plant more crops. By the second week their corn and potatoes were sprouting."

("Lesson 41: The Saints Settle the Salt Lake Valley," 238)

Today, if we wanted to sustain our families in a new, permanent home without relying on seed catalogs and stores, we'd face a stumbling block the pioneers never imagined. Few modern gardeners know that the vast majority of the seed we buy can never be used to produce true seed for the future.

Over the past century, vegetable seed has changed dramatically in ways previously unknown in the history of the world, thanks to modern technology. The seed the pioneers carried in 1847 is what we today call open-pollinated. The value of this kind of seed is simple: farmers and gardeners could save a portion of the year's seed crop to plant the next year.

Today, much of the seed used around the world is hybrid, meaning that if you take a seed from your garden, that seed will likely be sterile or produce fruit that does not resemble the parent. Such seed requires home gardeners to purchase new seed each season and removes the ability to provide our own seed from year to year.

Hybrid seed has been called a miracle and rightly so. Hybrids were developed to efficiently feed the world, and they have done so remarkably well for almost ninety years. Hybrid seed is valued for what scientists call vigor—that is, highly uniform crops. In recent years, new hybrids have been invented to make crops immune to certain herbicides and pesticides. These are valuable traits when the goal is to efficiently feed the world through mass production.

For the home gardener, hybrid seed has made seed-saving a challenge. The pioneers grew their own seed, but modern gardeners have little choice but to buy seed each year, even as the price of seed outpaces inflation. Some vendors have stopped labeling hybrid seed as such because it is now so common. One industrial seed producer has sued dozens of farmers who saved hybrid corn seed they had grown in their own fields.

Some would argue that in a pinch, we can simply revert to the way things were in pioneer times. But the massive shift to hybrid seed largely quashes the home gardener's ability to self-sufficiently grow their own seed.

In the West and across the nation, some gardeners have begun working to increase the availability of open-pollinated seed, allowing interested home gardeners to renew the self-provident gardens of the pioneer age.

"Bill of Particulars" (1845)

For the emigrants leaving this government next spring.
Each family consisting of five persons, to be provided with—

1 good strong wagon well covered with a light box.
2 or 3 good yoke of oxen between the age of 4 and 10 years.
2 or more milch cows.
1 or more good beefs.
3 sheep if they can be obtained.
1000 lbs. of flour or other bread, or bread stuffs in good sacks.
1 good musket or rifle to each male over the age of twelve years.
1 lb. powder.
4 lbs. lead.
1 do. Tea.
5 do. coffee.
100 do. sugar.
1 do. cayenne pepper.
2 do. black do.
½ lb. mustard.
10 do. rice for each family.
1 do. cinnamon.
½ do. cloves.
1 doz. nutmegs.
25 lbs. salt.
5 lbs. saleratus.
10 do. dried apples.
1 bush. of beans.

A few lbs. of dried beef or bacon.
5 lbs. dried peaches.
20 do. do. pumpkin.
25 do. seed grain.
1 gal. alcohol.
20 lbs. of soap each family.
4 or 5 fish hooks and lines.
15 lbs. iron and steel.
A few lbs. of wrought nails.
One or more sets of saw or grist mill irons to company of 100 families.
1 good seine and hook for each company.
2 sets of pulley blocks and ropes to each company for crossing rivers.
From 25 to 100 lbs. of farming and mechanical tools.
Cooking utensils to consist of bake kettle, frying pan, coffee pot, and tea kettle.
Tin cups, plates, knives, forks, spoons, and pans as few as will do.
A good tent and furniture to each 2 families.
Clothing and bedding to each family, not to exceed 500 pounds.
Ten extra teams for each company of 100 families.

N. B.—In addition to the above list, horse and mule teams can be used as well as oxen. Many items of comfort and convenience will suggest themselves to a wise and provident people, and can be laid, in season; but none should start without filling the original bill.

(*Nauvoo Neighbor*, October 29, 1845)

"Farmer Who Lied in Dispute with Monsanto Will Go to Prison"
St. Louis Post-Dispatch, May 7, 2003

A farmer opposed to Monsanto Co.'s genetic seed licensing practices was sentenced Wednesday in federal court at St. Louis to eight months in prison for lying about a truckload of cotton seed he hid for a friend.

Kem Ralph, 47, of Covington, Tenn., also admitted burning a truckload of seed, in defiance of a court order, to keep Monsanto from using it as evidence in a lawsuit against him.

The prison term for conspiracy to commit fraud is believed to be the first criminal prosecution linked to Monsanto's crackdown on farmers it claims are violating agreements on use of the genetically modified seeds.

Ralph pleaded guilty in U.S. District Court on Feb. 21 of lying in a sworn statement in the civil case.

At issue is seed-saving, the age-old agricultural practice of keeping seed from one crop to plant another. Monsanto's licensing agreement forbids it, a policy that has drawn bitter opposition from some farmers.

In court Wednesday, U.S. District Judge Richard Webber ordered Ralph to serve the prison time and to repay Monsanto $165,649 for about 41 tons of genetically engineered cotton and soybean seed he was found to have saved in violation of the agreement.

Monsanto says it has filed 73 civil lawsuits against farmers in the past five years over this issue.

Officials of the company, based in Creve Coeur, hoped that Ralph's case would send a stern message. Monsanto has distributed information about it and about the civil litigation as a warning.

Before Ralph's sentencing Wednesday, a Monsanto official told Judge Webber that other farmers would closely watch the outcome.

"Their behavior will be set according to the results here today," said Scott Baucum, an intellectual property protection manager for Monsanto.

The ruddy-faced Ralph appeared in court in blue jeans and a plaid shirt. He made no comment during or after the hearing. His attorneys have asked him to hold his peace because his civil case with Monsanto—in which he has already been ordered to pay more than $1.7 million to the agribusiness giant—is still not over.

But Ralph has been outspoken about his feelings. He said in a deposition in 2000 that opposition to Monsanto led to his decision to burn the bags of seed.

"Me and my brother talked about how rotten and lowdown Monsanto is. We're tired of being pushed around by Monsanto," he said then. "We are being pushed around and drug down a road like a bunch of dogs. And we decided we'd burn them."

Monsanto's new seeds have won widespread acceptance among American farmers. An example is genetically modified soybean seeds, which are designed to work with Monsanto's herbicide Roundup.

The seeds, which won government approval in 1994, are expected to account for 80 percent of the 73 million acres of soybeans planted in 2002 and 2003, the Department of Agriculture says.

Monsanto and its supporters say its fees are justified so the company can recoup costs and pay for future research.

Farmers who refuse to pay the fees obtain an unfair advantage over others, Monsanto says.

continues on page 7

continued from page 6

Some critics contend that the company's pricing is excessive and too tough on farmers.

"Farmers were always able to compete by saving seed. It's really a question of the corporate profit—that's what's being protected. If you can't save seed, you've got to buy it," said Lou Leonatti, an attorney from Mexico, Mo., who represents Ralph in his civil case.

People from Tipton County, near Ralph's home, wrote to tell Judge Webber that farmers there had suffered some hard years.

Paul D'Agrossa, attorney for Ralph in the criminal case, argued for probation so his client could continue to work the soil and support his teenage son.

But Webber, who explained that he had saved seed on the family farm where he grew up, said he could not ignore Ralph's efforts to conceal evidence.

"I'm not interested in making an example of Mr. Ralph. At the same time, I can't turn a blind eye to his conduct," the judge said.

Taking note of the planting season, Webber said he would not require the farmer to report to prison before July 1.

Pioneer Anson Call "had always been a successful farmer and in this locality his good fortune did not desert him though at first he met with some reverses. His oxen were poor and his cows helped to plow the new soil. . . . In the cricket plague of 1848–9 he succeeded in saving most of his crops gathering two hundred bushels of small grain from five bushels of seed also quite a crop of corn. In the harvest of 1850 he gathered a thousand bushels."

("Anson Call" *History of Utah: Biographical*)

W ithout seed catalogs and nurseries, the pioneers supplied themselves with year-round garden produce by using open-pollinated seed grown at home and in the community.

Open-pollinated seed in the garden is the vegetable equivalent of wheat in food storage. This pioneer solution is still possible today, and an increasing number of home gardeners are beginning to seek the benefits of preparedness and affordability inherent in traditional open-pollinated seed.

Our human debt to open-pollinated seed is evident in history. Wheat ended the need for societies to continuously roam in search of wild food. Wheat perfectly self-pollinates, meaning that wheat flowers naturally bear pure seed without any human intervention. The discovery of wheat meant populations could farm, saving seed from year to year to feed themselves. Like wheat, lettuce and beans also have perfect flowers, allowing easy seed saving—as long as the original seed is open-pollinated and not hybrid.

Purple-podded pole beans are allowed to dry on the vine, producing seed for the coming year. Beans are one of the few vegetable crops which can be counted on to produce seed with little or no natural crossing.

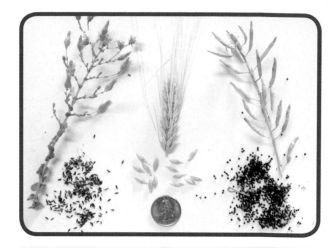

Garden seed and seed stalks from the author's garden (left to right): Lettuce seed stalk and cleaned seed, barley stalk and seed kernels, extra-dwarf pak choi stalk and seeds. The author was the first person in the world to offer pure extra-dwarf pak choi seed on Seed Savers Exchange. A quarter is show for size comparison.

In the same way, seed potatoes quelled mass starvation. Setting aside a small portion of potatoes to grow the next year meant food security—potatoes were simply cut into sections and sprouted to grow an abundant new crop.

Not all vegetables are so accommodating, however. To protect themselves against starvation due to seed shortages, the pioneers relied on an informal community seed bank, a tradition extending back thousands of years in human history. The need for this seed bank is rooted in the understanding of how seed grows.

Carrots, beets, turnips, onions, and most other root vegetables require two years to produce true seed. Carrots sprout from seed the first year, become dormant over winter, and then mature the second year to set seed. The loss of a year's carrot crop to pests, drought, theft, natural disaster, or desperation for food meant the loss of seed for the coming year—and thus potential starvation. Crop loss was especially dangerous because growing even a small amount of new seed from a few saved carrots took two years. In these situations, the informal pioneer seed bank was crucial because it allowed pioneers to trade or borrow seed to fend off starvation.

Carrot seed can also become useless by contamination. During pollination, the carrot flower must be kept isolated for purity because rogue pollen causes new seed to revert either immediately or over several generations to unwanted characteristics—shriveled, bitter roots. Most vegetables cross easily with one another like this, meaning you'll get strange fruit bearing little or no resemblance to the parent. Volunteer squash are a good example of the surprises you get when crossing occurs.

Throughout history, skilled gardeners and farmers not only fed nations by growing pure seed each year, they made the human eating experience more healthful and tasty by developing new kinds of fruit and vegetables. By skillfully selecting from natural plant crosses, larger carrots could be grown. Carrots were made sweeter, and new colors were introduced, including the orange carrot in the seventeenth century. Every vegetable we eat today was improved over centuries of work, not only by keeping pure seed lines alive, but also by inventing new seed lines.

Learn from the Pioneers

The First Year Pioneer Garden: 1848

My wife's great-great-grandfather, John Alma Vance, and thirteen members of his family arrived in Salt Lake Valley on Monday, Oct. 4, 1847. Over the next year, his journal records their struggle to remain optimistic in the face of looming starvation as crickets ate their crops and frost destroyed a succession of plantings. His journal expresses his joy at the first harvest, the fear of the community as the crops seemed on the brink of failure, and his determination to put his faith in his fields.

Though it is stated nowhere in the journal, the purpose of his writing is clear: he is charting every planting and harvest as a road map. John's journal is a rare, unvarnished look at the agricultural shock the pioneers confronted—the planting conditions were vastly different than they had experienced before. As a result, they planted too early and precious seed rotted.

Almost immediately after the Saints arrived, Brigham Young sent a group of men to California to purchase seed for crops. In John's journal, references to "California" seed refer to the seed that expedition returned with. I have included excerpts from John's journal detailing what the pioneers were planting, their struggle to figure out the local climate and growing season, and their desperation in the face of the cricket hordes.

On the day he entered the valley, John Vance wrote:

Rolled down canyon 4 miles to valley, and 4 to fort. So here in the valley of the Great Salt Lake. Good, all pleased, all right, all well . . . " But this sense of well-being was quickly tempered with the reality of preparing for winter. That evening, John wrote: "Called family together, presented the idea of dividing into three heads, self, Isaac and Wardsworth, also dividing the provisions according to size and number, that each might economize for itself and thereby effect a saving of breadstuffs, as it was short in consequence of the Pioneers having made nothing. All was agreed, so Tu. 5th opened last barrel of meal, divided between self, Isaac and Wardsworth in the following proportions:

Self - 6 ¾ lbs
Isaac - 2 ¾ lbs
Wardsworth - 2 ½ lbs

1848

Jan. 14-15: "Sowed 2 acres wheat 110 lbs"

Jan 18: "Sowed mustard, lettuce and onion seeds"

Apr. 13: "Congregation voted to authorize the high council to levy a tax to feed the poor"

Apr. 27: "This week has been cold, nights especially. Found and used water greens. Brother Shed poisoned by a root and died. Self, Wardsworth and boys swapped 60 pounds corn for wheat."

Mar. 2: "Sowed turnips, millet peas, parsnips, onions, sweet pepper, etc. Very warm."

continues on page 12

continued from page 11

Mar. 5: "This week has all been pleasant days and nights. Mustard and lettuce up. 40 men pursued Indians, returning today."

Mar. 7: "Sowed California wheat for self 50 lbs; for Wardsworth 15 lbs and Isaac 26 lbs."

Mar. 10: "Planted squash garden, California peas, bans and reddish turnips and onions."

Mar. 13: "Planted 7 rows of California peas."

Mar. 16: "Sowed millet, buckwheat and flaxseed."

Mar. 23: "Swapped 55 lbs corn to Br. Grant for wheat, same weight."

Mar. 25: "Onions coming up in first sowing."

Apr. 2: "Peas up."

Apr. 3: "Sent 87 lbs corn to mill in sacks, received same day by Wardsworth 85 lbs meal in sack."

Apr. 4: "Boys dig onions."

Apr. 5: "Sowed 3 rows sage and onions, gourds in field, sweet peppers, four rows of California peas."

Apr. 6: "Jim and self (plant) large bed onions, 10 rows peas."

Apr. 9: "Many discouraged about wheat. All seems right to me."

Apr. 14–15: "Planted 4 rows potatoes, 10 in row, three rows pale red and 1 blue N. Found California beans killed by frost; replanted in garden. Also planted 2 rows California beans on farm and last of the California peas."

Apr. 18: "Flax and buckwheat coming up; millet sprouted."

Apr. 19: "Corn coming up in garden. Plant beets."

Apr. 21: "Planting in E. garden or field, California beans and white beans 2 rows, four corn, sweet corn, California or Pueblo corn, flaxseed, Jumbo or Meridian corn, big long grapes and coffee, peas, watermelon and squash. Pleasant and growing weather. All this week no frost nights, except on Friday there was a little, none to hurt beans or corn."

Apr. 23: "50 lbs flour from mill, 59 of wheat taken."

Apr. 25: "Planted broad short grained corn next to road, then long grain, pumpkins, melon, popcorn, etc."

Apr. 26: "Squash, corn ,beets, parsnips, radish etc peas all up and California beans in garden also up."

May 2: "Cold and high wind at night. Hard frost killed beans, buckwheat and bent down corn."

May 14: "Some corn planted, flax sowed."

May 19-20: "Sowed in millet and buckwheat . . . Indian excitement."

May 23: "Planted on Red Bute farm, beans, melons, squash, cucumbers and rice corn."

May 25: "James and I planted beans and pumpkin seeds on Cam'l farm."

May 26: "Planted radishes in garden. Some heads of wheat showing. Some considerable complaint of crickets."

May 28: "Frost bean, potatoes and vines killed."

May 29: "Great alarm about crickets and frost, some wheat injured by it."

June 2: "My Red Bute farm laid low by crickets, though passed on, and the corn coming up again."

June 5: "Parley preached encouraging the people to hold on—we will make grain notwithstanding the crickets. This is the place for the Saints at present. Father Smith said 'You who have many cows, lend to those who have none, till harvest and then crickets will quit and we shall have plenty.' "

June 9: "Thousands of crickets."

June 11: "Plowed city garden, wheat all shooting out heads. Crickets devouring same. Many discouraged though cease not their exertions in watering and driving crickets. I still feel that enough will be left."

June 17: "Crickets devouring corn. Much alarm with some."

June 18: "Self and boys repair to Red Bute farm; drive

continues on page 13

continued from page 12

crickets out of wheat; corn all gone, or almost so."

June 19–20: "Replant 3½ acres and plant beans."

June 21–22: "Replanted city garden, planted last beans in same."

June 24: "Corn in tassle, crickets not so plenty. Peas for dinner."

June 26–27: "Finished watering fall wheat."

July 2: "Crickets quite plenty in wheat though seem not to notice corn or beans so much, some (settlers) cut a little, wheat prospects good. People better composed."

July 9: "Peeled some heads of wheat, rubbed out, ground and eat."

July 11: "Cut 20 lbs wheat by sickle."

July 12: "Eat the last bread of old stock."

July 20: "Everybody harvesting wheat, thrashing and eating."

Aug. 8: "Thrashed wheat."

Aug. 10: "Feast."

Aug. 17: "This week 5 sugar mills in operation, some little molasses made. Self made ½ gallon."

Aug. 26: "Ground corn stalks, made 3 gallons molasses."

Aug. 28: "Gathered May peas. Buckwheat making grain. Roasting ears in Caml field."

Sept. 3: "Cloudy and cool and mountains covered with new snow. Much fear of frost. My big corn frozen. Tender roasting ears back to most tender shoots clear of worms, and no frost. Joy."

1849

Jan. 15: "Shelled out corn 680 lbs 180 wheat."

Feb. 9: "Ground 30 lbs Spanish corn by handmill. Bishop number the people over one year and also ascertain amount of breadstuff when apportioned is ¾ lb to the person."

Feb. 11: "Meeting again in fort. Rich feast from Brigham. Unanimous vote to sustain each other in food like brethren and Christians."

1850

Nov. 8: "Planted fruit seed; 20 peach seed in box; next well and house corners staked—3 plum, walnut, hickory nut in same, 75 peach kernels in row next house; 100 (unreadable) seed in second row; 150 in third row and 150 in forth; also a gourd seed at each end of four corners."

(John Alma Vance was born in Tennessee in 1794 and died in Salt Lake City in 1882.)

A female pumpkin flower. The sex of the bloom can be discerned by the immature fruit on the stem. Pumpkin flowers can be as big as dinner plates.

CHAPTER 4

GROWING PURE SEED

Pioneer Julian Moses "secured a farm of about one hundred and twenty acres which he cultivated with skill and success. He had few equals in this line of industry year after year during times of scarcity caused by the ravages of crickets and grasshoppers. He furnished seed grain to his less successful neighbors for miles around. He made it a rule to have at least a two years' supply of grain on hand."

("Julian Moses" *History of Utah: Biographical*)

To grow pure seed today, the home gardener has the same four options used by every farmer and gardener over millennia.

1. PURE SEED THE EASY WAY

Open-pollinated wheat, lettuce, and beans self-pollinate perfectly, with no help needed from a gardener or farmer. This makes it possible to save seed even when you've grown three kinds of lettuce side by side, all flowering at the same time. Some minimal crossing is possible but most gardeners don't consider this to be a significant problem.

No seed is required to grow potatoes, so hybrid seed is not an issue with this vegetable. Potato plants do produce flowers and can produce seed, but the seed is unreliable and unnecessary. The potatoes themselves are cut into pieces to sprout new potato plants. Home-grown potatoes can be saved from year

"Yukon Gold"-variety potatoes grown in a straw bed in the author's garden. Growing potatoes in straw, rather than soil, is sometimes referred to as the "French method" and can be a great way to boost the potato harvest in clay soils.

Potatoes

Any homegrown potato can be stored for use as seed. To save potatoes for seed, store them in a cellar or other cool, dark place. Darkness is essential when storing potatoes. Exposure to light will cause potatoes to sprout prematurely, and then rot. When you are ready to plant the potatoes the next year, use only the best potatoes. Cut the larger potatoes into chunks with at least one potato "eye" (dimple) per chunk. Allow these to dry in direct sunlight for a day. At this point, they are ready to plant. Smaller potatoes, about the size of an egg, can be planted whole; because they are not cut open, no drying is necessary.

Lettuce

Only open-pollinated lettuce is useful for seed-saving, so be sure the seed you grow is labeled as open pollinated and not hybrid. Allow several lettuce plants to remain unharvested in the garden. Eventually, these plants will begin to grow flower spikes, usually during the heat of the summer. Natural pollination will occur and seeds will form. When the plants begin to turn yellow and die, seeds will be ready to harvest. Or allow seeds to self-scatter. Some will sprout on their own the next spring.

Beans

Only open-pollinated bean plants are useful for seed-saving. Beans come in two types: vine plants or bush plants. This method works for both. Allow several bean pods to remain unharvested in the garden. When the pods wither and dry up in autumn, seeds will be ready to harvest.

Store all seeds in paper envelopes in a cool, dry, dark place, secured from pests. For detailed information, read *Seed to Seed: Seed Saving and Growing Techniques for Vegetable Gardeners* by Suzanne Ashworth. Ashworth gives detailed instructions, often with photos, for saving seed from a whopping 160 different vegetables.

to year to grow new potatoes; these are commonly called seed potatoes. Store-bought potatoes should not be used because they are often treated to retard sprouting and are more likely to rot than produce a potato plant.

2. HAND POLLINATION

This method is the most useful for saving seed from plants prone to contamination. Contamination happens when unwanted natural pollination from cousin species—rogue pollen—enters the flower. Hand pollination can be quickly learned by even the least experienced growers. And it's fun! My four-year-old grandson loves to hand-pollinate summer squash with me.

Summer squash is the easiest plant to hand pollinate. Take a green zucchini, for example. Telling the difference between the male and female zucchini flowers is simple to learn. The female flower has a tiny, round, baby squash just below the flower, and the male flower does not. Next time you are out in your garden, poke around in your zucchini and see for yourself. If pollen from the male flower of any summer squash or cousin within the same species

Male and female squash blossoms. The male blossom, above, can be discerned from the female blossom, below, by looking for the immature fruit. The blossom above goes from flower to stem, while the female below features a blossom, immature yellow fruit, and green stem. Squash blossoms are among the easiest to sex, making them excellent for gardeners who are new to hand-pollination.

enters the female flower, the baby squash will grow.

Here is the challenge. If only pollen from other green zucchini enters the flower, the seeds of the squash that grows will be true seed and will produce more green zucchini. But if any of the pollen that enters the flower is from cousin species, the new seed will grow only mutant squash, bearing no resemblance to the parent.

Male pollen from an acorn squash, cocozelle, crookneck, many gourds, scallop squash, vegetable marrow squash, or any of the many other kinds of

How-To

How to Pollinate Summer Squash by Hand

For the home gardener looking to grow their own true green zucchini seed, here is a step-by-step explanation of how I hand pollinate zucchini. This works with all summer squash. A slightly different process, beyond the scope of this example, is used for pumpkins and winter squash.

- To begin, I identify which flowers on the green zucchini plant are approaching sexual maturity. Using immature flowers will fail to produce seed. Summer squash flowers signal they are approaching

continues on page 18

sexual maturity by beginning to turn yellow. This will happen the evening before the flower opens the next morning. In the evening, I find these flowers, both male and female, and use masking tape to tightly seal the tips so they cannot open in the morning. For best results, each male flower should be from a different plant. All plants should be the same variety of zucchini. Never mix cousin plants.

- The next morning, I snip the sealed male flowers from the plant with several inches of stem.
- I carefully remove the tape and petals from two or three male flowers to expose the anther of the male flower. The anther will be naturally coated in dusty yellow pollen.
- I pinch or tear off the tape from the tip of a single female flower. The rest of the flower will slowly open, revealing the yellow stigma of the female flower.
- Like an artist holding a paint brush, I hold the stem of one of the male flowers I've prepared and gently rub the pollen-covered anther on each section of the stigma. Or I let my four-year-old grandson, Xander, do this step, with my supervision.
- For a higher success rate, Xander and I use another one or two prepared anthers to swab the same female flower.
- With a new piece of masking tape, I close and tightly seal the petals of the female flower.
- I tie red yarn to the stem of the female flower below the baby fruit to mark the fruit so I can find it later.

- Over the next several days, I keep an eye on this female fruit. If my hand pollination was successful, the flower wilts down and disappears as the squash begins to grow. If I failed to pollinate the flower the flower will wilt, and the baby fruit will shrivel and die.
- Now I wait. The hand-pollinated fruit grows until large and fully mature. I know the squash is mature when the skin of the zucchini is hard enough to resist being dented by my fingernail. If you have chickens, take all means necessary to keep them out of the squash patch, because they will peck the growing fruit open and ruin it. Can you tell I'm speaking from experience on this one?
- I cut the mature zucchini and store in a cool, dark place for several week, but no longer than a month. At this point, I cut open the squash and remove the seeds. I dry the seeds indoors, out of direct sunlight, usually on a sheet of wax paper on top of the microwave (I don't know why—it just seems like a safe place). The seeds dry completely over several days.
- I keep the dried seeds in a paper envelope labeled with the name of the seed. I store my envelopes in a cool, dark place, usually a bureau drawer.

The next year, I plant the seeds just like they are store-bought seeds. If I'm lucky, they produce green zucchini, and then I know I made pure seed. Squash seeds will keep for several years, so I don't have to gather seeds from zucchini again for a while.

zucchini will result in a mutant squash instead of a perfect green zucchini.

Here is another challenge. Telling male and female zucchini apart may be simple, but distinguishing between male and female watermelon flowers is almost impossible, and this is true of many other vegetables. If you are like me and this kind of challenge does not dishearten you, start with the easiest vegetables—summer squash—and work your way up to more difficult varieties. Step-by-step instructions for hand-pollinating different species of vegetables are beyond the scope of this book. For expert guidance, I recommend *Seed to Seed* by Suzanne Ashworth.

3. ISOLATION BY TIME

Some very early-growing vegetables can be used for growing seed. I save seed from extra-dwarf pak choi, which is a mini version of bok choi. Pak choi is a fast-growing type of green, three to four

(left to right) An Italian variety of beet called chioggia, which features alternating rings of red and white when cut open. A Boule d'Or turnip, which is among the sweetest and most delicately flavored of all turnips but does not store for winter. A common purple-top turnip, which features the historic turnip taste and stores well into March and April when stored properly in a root cellar or garage.

inches tall. This plant will cross with turnips, some broccoli varieties, and Chinese cabbage, as well as other choi plants. But extra-dwarf pak choi has an advantage—speed. This plant grows so early and sets seed so quickly that others in this group, including early broccoli, have not gone to seed yet. So I feel comfortable saving the seed my extra-dwarf pak choi produces, as it is unlikely to be polluted by unwanted cousin pollen.

A yellow-stalked Swiss Chard from the "Bright Lights" chard variety. The succulent, tender leaves come early in spring and can be grown in a compost-heated cold-frame even in February. Swiss chard makes wonderful sauteed greens, and tastes great shredded in omelets.

I also save seed from an extremely fast-growing kind of open-pollinated corn, called Triple Play. This corn tassels out for pollination much earlier than even other rapid-growing varieties of corn. With research and experimentation, you may find other vegetables that you can successfully grow by species isolation.

4. ISOLATION BY DISTANCE

This method is useless for home gardeners. Here's why.

Chioggia beets boast red- and white-striped flesh and delicious flavor. Other kinds of beets are bright red, dark red, pure white, good for making sugar, or

good for winter storage. To keep these traits intact from one generation of seed to the next, the pollen of different beets cannot be mixed. Growing chioggia beets far away from any other beets is one way to make sure you grow pure seed.

The problem is, beets are wind pollinated. Studies have shown that beet pollen can travel up to five miles. If a dark red beet produces pollen at the same time as the chioggia beet, and within five miles, both beets could produce seed that will grow beets that do not resemble the parents. Of course this is only if the original beets were grown from open-pollinated seed. If the beets are hybrid, the new seed could be sterile or produce beets with no resemblance to the parents—shriveled or bitter beets, for example.

For those of us who don't live on a huge farm, trying to control what is planted around us for five miles is laughable. You can't feasibly go door to door and announce that you are growing beets this year, so no one else within five miles should grow beets unless they are of the exact variety you are growing. Isolation by distance is great for huge farms, but not feasible for the rest of us.

To make the matter more complicated, garden beets are direct relatives of sugar beets, mangels (a type of huge beet historically fed to livestock), and Swiss chard. This means that any of these could also pollinate our chioggia beet during pollination, creating useless seed.

CHAPTER 5

THE PIONEER SEED-SAVING SOLUTION

"Agreeable to President Young's instructions, Elder Pratt, accompanied by George A. Smith, John Brown, Joseph Mathews, John Pack, Orrin Porter Rockwell, and J. C. Little, started on this morning on horses to seek out a suitable place to plant some potatoes, turnips, etc., so as to preserve the seed at least."

(William Clayton Journal, July 22, 1847)

As home gardeners, none of us can keep up continuous lines of pure seed for all strains of vegetables and grains—such a feat simply isn't possible.

The pioneers had an elegantly simple solution to all this—what I call the pioneer community seed bank. For them, trading seed was routine. They were, in essence, their own seed store.

If one family had a certain bean variety and another family had a squash seed, they could trade. One farmer had a fondness for a certain melon from the old country, while another perpetuated a line of corn or potatoes. Seeds were bartered, traded, sold, and given away. There are numerous pioneer accounts of farmers both carefully storing up seed year after year, and other accounts farmers losing their crop and turning to neighbors for the new seed necessary to start over again the next year.

Learn from the Pioneers

"In March (1848) was a very pleasant spell of winter. On the tenth William Matthews planted his corn, urged me to plant my morsel of seeds, but as our next year's bread depended on the good use made of the few kernels of corn, I waited. A cold spell of weather set in, April, and Mr. Matthews seed corn rotted in the ground. He had other seed corn to supply and plant a second time and a third time replanted the same patch and he was put out with my slow actions. My corn ground was ploughed ready waiting for one month and on the 10th day of May, I planted the long saved seed. It soon sprouted and came up. It grew finally and to my surprise began to shoot near the ground as I never saw Spanish corn grow before, and had from six to eight ears to the hill, and we had sufficient for bread for three families."

("Kartchner, Wiliam Decatur" *Our Pioneer Heritage*)

This "seed bank" method was not invented by the pioneers. The seed bank was commonly used the world over before the twentieth-century industrialization of seed production. Many of immigrants to the West brought seed with them from their native countries, seed that had been favored and passed down for generations, and was considered too important to leave behind. Some of those rare heirloom strains still survive within families. Across the nation, a few have even been rescued from extinction when a stash of decades-old seed has been found in a grandparents' deep freezer and then carefully cultivated for preservation. Most, however, have clearly been lost to extinction.

A community seed bank really only exists as a community project. The work of actually saving pure seed from year to year in the home garden is a powerful demonstration of what we have been given by our ancestors and what we have given up as some open-pollinated vegetables have died out through disuse.

THE NEW SEED BANK

In 1975, Diane Ott Whealy's terminally ill grandfather gave her and her husband, Kent Whealy, the seeds of two heirloom garden plants—a flower variety and a pink-fleshed tomato from Germany, brought over by his parents from Bavaria when they immigrated to St. Lucas, Iowa, in the 1870s. Struck by the gift they had been given, and recognizing that if they did not continue the line both varieties would quickly be lost, the Whealys founded Seed Savers Exchange in 1975. They didn't know it then, but the couple had single-handedly started a small volunteer movement to save what remained of the world's homegrown, open-pollinated seed. Much of this seed is available nowhere else.

Today, 11,000 members around the world participate in the nonprofit Exchange, and have mailed over one million seed samples to one another. Many of the seeds offered were once sold commercially but have been discontinued and would have been lost without private gardeners keeping the seed lines alive.

In 2010, the members offered 13,571 varieties of open-pollinated, privately grown vegetable seed, including more than 4,600 kinds of tomatoes and 1,400 types of beans. The Exchange is a worldwide, Internet version of the community seed bank network that once existed in every country in the world before hybrid seed was invented in the 1920s.[1]

When I finally joined the exchange in 2009, I anticipated finding local gardeners working to

This pioneer root cellar fed the family of George Henry and Ann Elizabeth Gubler for many years, and still exists in Lund, Nevada, after being abandoned for half a century. Cellaring was the key to self-sufficient fresh food storage for the family before daily trips to the grocery store. The author is one of very few who still use this skill.

preserve the Mormon pioneer seed heritage. Given the history of seed-saving in Utah, the historic emphasis on gardening in the LDS Church, and the sheer number of pioneer families that brought seed to the West from all over the world, I was ready to join Utah's thriving community of heirloom seed savers. Imagine my double take when I opened my Seed Savers Exchange directory to find I was only the fifth Utah resident to join that group.

I had turned to the Exchange in part because I had never been given any heirloom seed by my great-grandparents or grandparents. My parents were not gardeners—like many of their generation, they didn't need to be. In addition to the grocery store, our family was fully supplied with eggs, fresh raw milk, kitchen-churned butter, and myriad vegetables from grandparents and great-grandparents on both sides. My father raised beef cattle, and we always had a freezer full of meat.

We lived in a truly tiny pioneer farming burg in central Utah, a half-hour drive from even the smallest grocery store. Fast food was a rare extravagance, available only on rare shopping excursions "up north" to Salt Lake City. From childhood I gathered eggs with my grandmother and great-grandmother and routinely picked their backyard vegetables. In winter, I was sent to their basement storerooms for a home-canned jar of fruit or jelly, beans or beets, ketchup or pickles. The jars glistened in the dim light of the storeroom and made a delightful clink when jostled.

The storerooms of my grandparents on both sides of my family were modern compared to my great-grandmother's cavernous, cool underground storeroom made from local stone by my great-grandfather many decades before. How I loved that cellar! The damp-earth fragrance, the humid air, the natural warmth in winter, the colors of yellow wax beans, blood-red beets, golden peaches, dragon-fleshed green pickles with exotic herbs floating in the brine. Even as a child, my great-grandmother's cellar room represented security to me. Though it was not spoken, I knew our family would never want for food because my grandparents and great-grandmother were experts in garden alchemy. Year after year, they planted seeds in spring to fill plank shelves in autumn until those shelves groaned under a sea of glass jars. Wooden bins overflowed with huge potatoes, thick carrots, and bulbous, peeling onions.

My goal in joining with other gardeners to save and exchange seeds is to focus more on growing my own open-pollinated seed. With that seed, I am extending my garden harvest across the calendar as the pioneers had once routinely done.

Note

1. "About Us," seedsavers.org.

Put Away for Winter: One Utah Root Cellar

In her memoirs, my great-grandmother, Lexia Dastrup Warnock, 1890–1985, recalled, "We put carrots, red beets, turnips, and cabbage away for winter in the root cellar, away from frost . . . we dried corn when good for eating, then cooked it back tender to provide corn for winter time.

". . . the day had been long and wearying. Dozens of jars of red beets for winter eating were shining on the table."

Her journal entries also chronicled her self-reliant lifestyle; her generation was the last to primarily feed their families off their land:

Aug. 2, 1966: "Washed windows, weeded, etc. Built compost piles out of weeds."

Sept. 24, 1969: "We picked the blue damson plums from our tree. Very good. I put 18 quarts in the jars for future use."

Aug. 11, 1971: "Canned 10 pints of beets, 3 of beans."

Sept. 11, 1971: "Grandpa Haderlie came to Carl's bringing some tomatoes and pears. They went to work and canned 200 quarts of tomatoes that day."

My grandfather, Irvin Warnock, sang his wife's praises for her efforts at keeping the family fed in winter through preservation of the autumn harvest:

Sept 30 1971

"I think Mom has a sixth sense of autumn time. She can feel it in the air, or something. She spent this forenoon harvesting the carrots, and the balance of the potatoes, from the garden. There were three bushel baskets of carrots. (I surely hope that we two old cronies don't have to eat THAT many carrots this winter.) A total of eight baskets of potatoes all snugly stored in the old dirt cellar back of the shop."

His work for Sevier County "brought in the money which helped put the kids thru school and sent some of them on missions. Please note that I did not say it put any food on the table—that came from Mom's fertile garden, made possible by her hard work. Bless her!"

". . . We made a wonderful fruit cellar for Mom under the center of the house, nice and cool, nearly always a uniform temperature, where she can keep canned fruits and canned vegetables almost indefinitely. What I mean is that some of it gets kept TOO long. We have enough stuff stored down there to last us—not merely two years, as the Church advises, but clear thru the millennium."

On the 16th of November (1847), O. P. Rockwell, E. K. Fuller, A. A. Lathrop, and fifteen others set forth for California to buy cows, mules, mares, wheat, and seeds . . . During the autumn, several parties of the battalion men arrived from California, bringing a quantity of wheat. . . . Col Markham reported at this meeting "that 13 ploughs and 3 harrows had been stocked during the past week, 3 lots of ground broken up, one lot of 35 acres planted in corn, oats, buckwheat, potatoes, beans, and garden seed."

Bancroft, *History of Utah*, 1540–1886

A view of the author's garden, including greens which have gone to flower, turnips, onions, cabbage, broccoli, and peas. Eating fresh out of the garden doesn't have to require a lot of space, or a lot of time or effort.

THE CHALLENGE: EXTENDING THE HARVEST

To the self-sufficient home gardener, hardy vegetables promise fresh food in the dead of winter, without the aid of a root cellar, greenhouse, cold frame, or artificial heating.

In the garden, a "hardy" vegetable is any outdoor vegetable that can be eaten fresh in winter. Many actually develop a sweeter flavor after a few hard frosts. Vegetables that are not hardy are called tender, meaning they cannot survive frost and exposure to freezing temperatures.

Where I live, the normal garden harvest grinds to a halt in the last week of September, when the first frosts typically hit. Frost kills what's left of the tender summer vegetable plants. Tomato plants, for example, collapse and turn black when frozen overnight.

Extending the harvest into October, November, December, the New Year, and beyond means self-reliant families can provide more of their own food, spending less at the grocery store.

THE FALL CROP

By autumn, lettuce planted in spring has turned bitter, gone to seed, or been eaten. Past their prime, beets and turnips have turned fibrous in the heat. Planting a fall crop of tender vegetables gives the home gardener a second chance to eat these foods fresh before winter hits. This crop will not live beyond the prolonged freeze of winter, but they grow so rapidly that they can extend the season.

Fall crop vegetables (and suggested planting dates for the Rocky Mountain area):

- Bok choi and pak choi (August–September)
- Lettuce (August–September)
- Beets (early August)
- Turnips (early August)
- Broccoli (early August)
- Cabbage (early August)
- Radishes (August–September)
- Peas (mid-July–August)

Harvests will depend on the variety and Mother Nature. Choose the earliest-maturing vegetables available for fall planting. An early hard freeze can sometimes kill the autumn crop. Even hardy fall crops need to be fairly mature before the ground freezes, and an early hard frost can stunt their growth or kill the immature plants. *When it comes to fall crops, advanced planning is often crucial. Finding vegetable seed in August in the West is difficult, so plan out your fall crop in spring and purchase seed for fall at that time.*

Hardy Vegetables for Winter Harvest in the Home Garden

LETTUCE

Gardeners sometimes have difficulty believing that hardy lettuce can be anything but a prank. Lettuce, after all, is one of the most delicate vegetables in the garden—usually quick to be killed by frost, extremely sensitive to heat, quick to turn bitter without the right amount of water, and bolting—prematurely producing seed stalks—almost overnight when the thermometer climbs. For many commercial varieties,

---

For Your Information

Hardy vegetable: any outdoor vegetable eaten fresh from the garden in winter.
Tender vegetable: any vegetable plant that cannot survive frost and exposure to freezing temperatures.

Winter-type lettuces under snow in the author's garden in late October. Many vegetable varieties were bred for winter use centuries ago, but growing them has become a forgotten skill.

all this is true. But over the centuries, certain strains of lettuce have been developed specifically for winter use. In the United States and much of the world, these strains have long ago been abandoned because lettuce is now routinely shipped to grocery stores from locations around the world. Few home gardeners have actually grown winter lettuce.

But for those looking for the independence of being able to produce inexpensive winter lettuce at home, finding seed for the ancient varieties is still possible. And don't be fooled—winter lettuce is still succulent, crisp, and delicious. You'll be surprised at not only the taste but also the pleasure of serving a Sunday dinner salad straight from your December garden.

For Fall and Winter Lettuce

Seed Savers Exchange offers these cold-hardy varieties (plant in August):

- Brown Dutch Winter, a butterhead-type said

Baby lettuces have begun to grow in a compost-heated cold frame in September. Three feet of earth is removed from below the frame, and then two feet of green horse and chicken manure are put back in, followed by a foot of compost. Heat from the decomposing manure keeps the temperature of the cold-frame above freezing even on nights that hit 15 below zero.

(top) A close-up view of purple "Marvel of Four Seasons" winter lettuce on the left, with "Brown Goldring" winter lettuce on the right. Both varieties are among the most winter-hardy of all winter lettuces. (bottom left) Cabbages and peas in the early garden. (bottom right) Rows of "Brown Goldring" lettuce planted in August. The first lettuces were ready to eat on October 15 and stayed fresh in the garden without protection until Christmas.

to have been grown at Monticello by Thomas Jefferson. This lettuce is reported to overwinter without protection even in USDA Zone Four, with temperatures below freezing.

• Brown Winter is a bibb-type lettuce that, according to Exchange members, overwinters nicely even under snow cover and grows well in unheated cold frames or greenhouses in winter.

• Hanson, a crisp-head variety that withstands both heat and frost and grows up to five pounds.

• Winter Marvel, a butterhead-type lettuce that performs well outdoors in winter.

• Tango, a loose-leaf lettuce that performs well in winter, tolerates summer heat, and grows quickly.

• Brown Goldring, a romaine lettuce that performs well in my Utah garden, tastes great, is slow to react to heat, and is very cold hardy. This lettuce variety has even won awards. The only problem I had with it in my garden is that the deer liked it too!

• Another favorite of mine is "Marvel of Four Seasons" or "Lettuce Merveille des Quatre Saisons." This stunningly beautiful lettuce is named for its hardiness. An 1885 French heirloom, this butterhead variety has cranberry, green, and bronze-colored leaves so fantastic to look at that you almost hate to eat it. Almost.

For Spring and Summer Lettuce

Any open-pollinated lettuce can be started indoors in late winter for early spring planting, or planted directly in the garden in spring or fall. If you allow a handful of plants to go uneaten, they often self-seed, meaning the lettuce will plant itself in the garden and come up on its own the next year. For all practical purposes, this quality essentially turns self-seeding lettuce into a perennial vegetable. Fall-planted lettuces are great for eating but will not have enough time to go to seed.

Kale

Kale is renowned for its performance as a winter green. This large-leafed vegetable has been a reliable hunger gap food for centuries, and is highly nutritious. The leaves come in red, green, and blue colors and in straight- or curly-leafed varieties. The 2010 Seed Savers Exchange directory lists thirty-eight available varieties. In spring, you can take the immature flower shoots of over-wintered kale that you are not keeping for seed and eat them sautéed in butter or steamed.

Kohlrabi

This vegetable is always one of the most visually interesting in the garden at any time of year. The leaves are a bold purple and green, and as the plant matures, a large bulb spiked with leaves forms at the soil level. Members of Seed Savers Exchange offer just four varieties. This plant does well in summer heat (though it can lose its tenderness if left too long in the

A purple Kohlrabi plant. Kohlrabi are one of the most visually interesting vegetables in the fall garden. The leaves are removed and the round stem is sliced into salads or just eaten alone as a side-dish. Kohlrabi tastes like sweet broccoli, but gives off a terrible sulphur smell if kept in the house.

summer garden) or winter cold, keeps well for weeks in the fridge or cellar, and reportedly tastes great as a slaw. The leaves can be used for salad or greens. Cut into chunks, the flesh of the bulb is white inside and makes a great addition to a dish of roasted vegetables in winter. (See recipe in last chapter).

Cabbage

Seed Savers Exchange members offer up to forty-three varieties, many antique and most from outside the United States. They range from flat and grey-green to the green or purple globes common in grocery stores. Cabbage lasts many weeks in the fridge or months in the cellar. The leaves are great raw in salad, fried with sausage or beef, stuffed, pickled, slawed, or chopped. In our house we like to finely slice cabbage to serve on top of tacos instead of lettuce—the crunch adds a great texture. Cabbage has one great advantage over lettuce—it lasts much longer in the fridge. Leftover lettuce wilts and turns

A close-up of cabbages planted in August. The leaves can be eaten fresh or sauteed in winter. The cabbage head will be produced in early spring.

limp, but a head of cabbage can be sliced away slowly, to be used day after day, and still tastes as delicious and crunchy on the last day as it did the first. We also use cabbage in winter in place of lettuce on sandwiches or hamburgers.

Spinach

As they do with the hardy lettuces, most gardeners are astonished to learn that some heirloom spinach varieties perform very well in winter. Seed Savers Exchange members in 2010 offered eight cold-hardy varieties:

- America, a variety reported to have outperformed all others in an unheated greenhouse over winter in Pennsylvania. In my own garden, the plants suffered from the heat of summer, and not only were slow to grow but also extremely slow to bolt.
- Bloomsdale Long Standing, a small-leafed spinach that overwinters to produce well in spring.
- Bloomsdale Winter, a good fall and winter spinach with dark green leaves.
- Cold Resistant Savoy, resistant to both cold and heat, as well as slow to go to seed, a trait that provides a longer window for harvest.
- Guntmadingen Winter, a rare Swiss heirloom variety that is exceptionally winter hardy. Oak-leaf shaped leaves.
- Haldenstein, another Swiss variety named after a Swiss village that has been keeping this seed line alive since before the First World War. A great fall crop, winter spinach with large leaves.
- Norfolk, overwinters with mulch or some protection for a spring harvest, making it another food that helped to end the hunger gap in the days before industrialized food.
- Verdil, a giant-type spinach that Exchange members report as an excellent producer in winter, even under a foot of snow in Oregon.

Cabbages, winter-hardy spinach, and several varieties of winter lettuce planted in August in a grow box in the author's garden. The lettuces are circled with wire to keep the deer from feasting on them.

CHAPTER 7

SELF-SUFFICIENCY USING GARDEN BOXES

Garden boxes give two advantages to the provident family—far less weeding, and the ability to guarantee stone-free soil for root crops. Here are things you should know when considering box gardening:

BUILD YOUR BOXES FOR FREE

I have eight garden boxes and have not paid a cent for any of them beyond buying screws at the hardware store. One neighbor couple gave me a pile of boards that had been sitting in their yard for many years, and I hastily turned these into foot-deep grow boxes for carrots, using only a small electric chain saw to rough-cut the lengths I wanted. Another friend gave me scrap wood from his work that the company would have otherwise had to pay to haul away to the landfill—a terrible waste of perfectly usable lumber. All you need to build your own boxes

Three-inch-tall grow boxes planted in August for fall crops. These boxes are surrounded by spring-planted boxes, which are full of summer's bounty.

is some old boards, some kind of saw, wood screws, and a screwdriver, preferably electric.

SAVE ON THE COST OF SOIL

The expensive part of grow boxes is filling them with soil, but boxes can be built in different depths for different vegetables. My foot-deep boxes are for carrots and parsnips. In my 4-inch-deep boxes, I grow onions and wheat during the summer, and during the fall, they are used for beets, turnip, chard, and more. My six-inch boxes have squash, peas, beans, tomatoes, short carrots, broccoli, and more.

When filling your boxes, there is no need to use expensive, specially packaged soils. If you have it, use your own homemade compost. Bags of steer manure mixed with compost are extremely inexpensive at about a dollar for a large bag. Bales of peat moss are low-priced and make a great garden box additive. Bulk garden compost is available by the cubic yard at low prices if you have access to a truck. The bottom of deeper boxes can be filled with leaves. The bottom of my straw-filled potato grow boxes are layered with raked up pine needles, which benefit potatoes as they break down over time. It costs me about fifteen dollars to fill the 16-foot-long, 3-foot-wide, 4-inch-deep box that I use for onions and wheat.

Gardening Tip

The Easiest Compost Ever

Here is a truly convenient way to compost household vegetable waste in winter—simply through it out onto the snow-covered garden each day. If you get regular snow, as we do, the garden will not be unsightly, and the freeze-thaw cycle begins to quickly break down the organic matter. The whole thing is then simply tilled under as you prepare for spring gardening.

To give my seeds the best sprouting conditions, I place a thin layer of a premium, inexpensive garden soil blend—less than an inch deep—across the entire surface of my grow boxes.

START SLOW

There is no reason to convert wholesale from a traditional backyard garden to box gardens. A box of stone-free soil for carrots or difficult-to-weed onions is a good jumping-off point for gardeners experimenting with box gardening. The vast majority of my garden is still traditional, but I'm converting more space to boxes each year, just because weed-free gardening is hard to resist.

ONE LARGE BOX OR MANY SMALLER BOXES?

I have seen gardeners build one very long, wide, deep garden box and bring in a dump truck-load of soil to fill it. I have watched these boxes become weedy in the center over time because they are too large to easily access the center space. I prefer long boxes, each about three feet wide, with a path between each box. To keep weeds out of your garden box pathways, lay down a layer of straw, or even strips of old carpet (earth-tone colors blend in nicely), or both.

WATERING

Many row-box users install drip irrigation systems, the cost of which can add up if you have a lot of box space. I have opted to attach an oscillating sprinkler, with a dedicated hose, to one of my center boxes, providing overhead watering for all the boxes at once. One caution: squash should not be planted where overhead watering occurs, as wet squash leaves are extremely prone to powder mildew and will succumb rapidly if exposed to repeat overhead watering.

(top left) A single overhead sprinkler screwed to a grow box filled with carrots waters all the boxes. (top right) French pumpkins in flower in front of fall-planted vegetable boxes. (bottom) The fall-planted boxes are blank compared to the garden around them.

A basketful of turnips, canteloupe, summer squash, beets, and more picked in the author's garden in August. The goal of the self-sufficient gardener is to spread the harvest across four seasons.

CHAPTER 8

GROWING PERENNIAL VEGETABLES

Perennial flowers are far better known in the garden than perennial vegetables, but there are some vegetables, especially some heirloom varieties, which return year after year without requiring the purchase of seed, or special care, from the gardener.

When used to describe garden plants, the word *perennial* means any plant that dies during winter but then comes up again each spring without help from the gardener. Perennials save time and money and ensure that even if your life gets so crazy that you can't even manage to get the garden planted in spring, you will still have at least a few fresh foods for your family.

SELF-SEEDING LETTUCE

This is by far my favorite perennial. A few years ago, I direct-sowed an open-pollinated butter crunch lettuce into my garden. The lettuce thrived in spring, producing an abundance of loose leaves for salads and sandwiches. But, as with most lettuces, once the heat of summer hit, the plants bolted (went to seed) quickly. Luckily, I never quite got around to cleaning up all of the plants that had gone to seed, and the next spring, and each spring following, I have

A single buttercrunch lettuce emerging from the soil in fall.

been presented with a new crop grown from the seed thrown down by the plants the previous summer. I was so happy that I actually expanded the lettuce patch. After all, what can beat a garden crop that plants itself, replants itself, and requires no fertilizer, no tilling, and no expensive seed?

Technically, *perennial* is a misnomer here, because my lettuce is not the same plant returning each spring, but the next generation seed planting itself. But whatever the mechanics may be, the result is perennial lettuce.

To extend the harvest even longer, collect some of the seed and sow it in mid-spring after the self-sown seed has sprouted. This will produce a second crop in late spring, which in my garden has continued to produce new lettuce without heat bitterness well into July. To further extend the harvest, spread some of your saved seed in a small vegetable bed under the deep shade of a mature tree for a crop of lettuce in July and August. A fourth crop can then be grown in the cool temperatures of autumn, and if you have set out winter hardy lettuce as discussed in the previous chapter, you now have fresh lettuce out of the garden for twelve months out of the year. Because lettuce

Egyptian Walking Onions are among the oldest perennial garden vegetables and were a staple and favorite of the pioneers. We know this because they are still found, often forgotten, in the ditch banks of many of the pioneer gardens that still exist today. These onions produce shallot bulbs at the top of their stem, rather than at the ground. When the stems fall over in autumn, the onions replant themselves.

is so easy to grow, it could easily become the first year-round garden vegetable for every gardener who is just beginning to experiment with a four-season backyard harvest.

WALKING ONIONS

Recently, a friend in her early thirties purchased an old home in the historic pioneer section of downtown Provo, Utah. In one corner of the backyard was a patch of earth crowded by an odd-looking plant left over from the previous owner. Waist-high, the green tube-like leaves resembled giant-sized green onions. They were topped with gnarled purple-brown domes and looked like a garden sculpture. I remarked that she was lucky to have inherited a mature patch of perennial Egyptian walking onions—I'd had to pay for my own walking onion starts from a grower in the mid-West.

"Walking what?" my friend asked.

Admittedly the name may sound like something from science fiction, but it is actually apropos. Walking onions are so-called because they form small bulbs—bulbils—at the top of their stalks and when those stalks finally fall over at the end of the season—"walk"—the bulbils plant themselves. The bulbils store well over winter for eating, and the stalks are used as green onions. The plants are extremely hardy, withstanding frigid winters and drought. And

A "Potato Onion," also known as a "Multiplier Onion." A single bulb, planted in spring, grows two to eight new bulbs.

because they require really no work on the part of the gardener, they are one of the few pioneer plants that are still actively passed down in families and among neighbors, though even this is declining because knowledge of this plant is fading from the public memory. They're also called spreading onions, topset onions, and winter onions.

MULTIPLIER ONIONS

Planted in the garden, a single small bulb of multiplier onion produces a prolific bunch of ground-level bulbs by the end of the season. This onion is fun to watch as it evolves over the summer season because as they divide, each new shallot-type bulb sends out a green stalk, and soon the plant looks like a botanical version of mythical Medusa's head. The bulbs have a wonderful aroma and store right up to the next summer. Several varieties offered by Seed Savers Exchange members have been directly passed from generation to generation for over a century, including one called Greeley Bunching documented as originally arriving in Kansas by covered wagon. They're also known as shallots, bunching onions, and potato onions.

DANDELIONS

Wait, don't flip the page!

Yes, reader, I can hear you muttering now—why on earth would you waste time on a weed, a yard pest you've been trying to get rid of? Nutrition is the reason. Dandelion greens are far and away more nutritious than lettuce or even other greens.

"But if that were true," you are saying, "we would be eating them instead of spraying them with weed killer."

We did eat them once. By "we" I mean our ancestors, both in this nation and throughout the world. In the days before grocery stores offered round-the-clock access to cellophane pillows of greens, dandelions were a prized food. To this day, dandelion greens are more common than lettuce in grocery stores around Italy. As mentioned in chapter one, few now remember that when the pilgrims arrived at Plymouth Rock, there were no dandelions dotting the United States. Emigrants brought them here and valued them for being the plant that broke the hunger gap each spring. In lean years, the hunger gap began in late winter when food cellars and winter vegetables had been used up and did not end until the first perennial greens—dandelions—appeared. Dandelions are also hugely important to the health of beehives, because they are the first flower to bloom each year in the West (with the exception perhaps of the crocus), and this is another reason pilgrims and settlers imported them to this country. Honeybees are among the first pollinators to emerge after winter each year, coming out to find food when daytime temperatures rise to 45 degrees. Like humans, honeybees too put up cellars of food—honeycombs—and hives also experience a hunger gap as those cellars run low, especially if those hives have been harvested (by humans) the previous fall. For both bees and pre-industrial people, the emergence of dandelions was a welcome sight because it meant food.

Dandelions can be eaten in two ways. Just as they emerge in spring, before they have set flowers, the greens are succulent and sweet for eating raw as salad. But as soon as those yellow tufts of flowers begin to appear, the leaves turn bitter. That bitterness vanishes completely once the dandelions are either steamed or sautéed. Beyond using early greens for salad, my favorite dandelion dish is to stuff them inside homemade rustic ravioli. I always make a large batch, using about a half-bushel of dandelion crowns (the tightly packed, white shoots immediately above the root) and greens (which reduce greatly when cooked). While the rest of the family prefers them topped with pasta sauce, I eat them for lunch with butter and Parmesan cheese and a glass of home-canned grape juice. We freeze the rest to eat later. Even frozen solid, they take only four or five minutes to cook in boiling water, making them a superb "fast food" for a wholesome family meal. Of course, be sure the dandelions you are using have not been treated with any kind of herbicide, even "drift" poison from your neighbors. And wash them thoroughly.

One final note on dandelions: If you are really in the mood to test your pioneer resolve, and you have vowed not to buy greens out of season at the grocery store, dandelions can be forced indoors in winter with very little effort. John Seymour gives complete instructions in his book, *The Self-sufficient Life and How to Live It*. If nothing else, it's a great family home evening pioneer living object lesson. You and the kids can peek in on the progress of the shoots from time to time, and in the end you get to eat your work.

A view of the author's perennial flower garden in fall, featuring Indian blanket flowers, cosmos, sunflowers, daylilies, purple coneflower, with a few annual zinnias and marigolds.

SWEET SELF-RELIANCE: GRAPES & FRUIT TREES

GRAPES

Grapes are one of the all-time favorite pioneer garden treats. Nothing could be easier to grow or taste better in winter preserves.

Grapes require no fertilizer and thrive even in the stony, alkaline soil that is the trademark of the West. The vines will likely outlive you, and they produce copious amounts of grapes even if you never get around to pruning them. If you do want to prune them, they are among the easiest backyard pruning jobs. Simply identify one or two main branches running the length of the fence or support your vines are on, and cut back everything else to about two feet in length. This severe pruning is necessary because grapes only grow on new canes each year.

To prevent disease on cut canes, grapes are pruned in January or February, when there is still snow on the ground and temperatures are chilly. For me, pruning the grapes is a great cure for cabin fever, one of those jobs I can't wait to get around to because I'm itching for the arrival of the garden season. And even a long row of vines takes only ten or twenty minutes to trim, so by the time your nose is frosty and red, you are done.

A bunch of Concord grapes beginning to blush with their final color in autumn. Hardy grapes need almost no attention to produce a huge volume of fruit. Grapevines often outlive their owners.

And grapes are free. Few people know anymore just how easy it is to start your own grape vine. There are two ways to propagate grapes. The easiest is to dig up a volunteer start—when a grape vine touches moist soil and takes root. If you don't have any volunteers, look for vines on or near the ground and put a shovelful of garden soil over a few inches of the vine, pinning it to the ground. If this cane is live wood (light brown instead of gray), then a new grape plant will likely sprout within a few weeks. Keep the soil moist, though.

If you don't have any grape vines in your yard, the second method may work well for you. Find a friend or neighbor with a vine and ask permission in January or February to cut off some vines—they need to be pruned off anyway, so you are really doing them a favor. Try to choose vines that are light brown and not gray, as the gray vines are dead wood. If you are not sure which is which, just choose from a selection of pruned vines. From these, cut six or eight pieces to the length of your forearm and stick them in a pot of soil, about an inch apart. Some sources suggest you use root hormone, available in any plant nursery, but I've never needed it.

The key to get the vines to sprout green leaves is to warm the soil while keeping the canes a little cooler. This can be done in several ways. Tie or tape a plastic bag, with a little water in it, around the pot (not around the branches!) and set the whole thing in a sunny window. Or use a seed tray heating pad, used to warm seed pots for starting in winter. I wrap a thin wool lap blanket around the pot and then set it on the seed tray warmer for about a week. Slightly warming the soil allows the grape canes to start sending out roots. After about a week, a light green nub will begin to swell out of the side of one or more canes. Over the next few days, this nub grows larger and larger, finally unfolding to become a pale green leaf about the size of a Kennedy half-dollar. At this point I turn off the seed tray warmer, remove the blanket, and keep the soil moist for several weeks.

I have started grapes canes in February and as late as days before the vines grow their own green nubs outside, in early April. By late April or early May, when the canes have several leaves, I set them in the afternoon sun for a couple of days to get them used to direct sunlight, bringing them into the house at night. And then I plant them right into the clay soil. Just like

A harvest of backyard grapes at the author's home. These grapes were turned into juice and jelly, and eaten throughout the winter and spring. The author and his family regularly put up more than 100 quarts of grape juice, and many dozens of grape jelly in shades of purple, white, and rose.

canes from the nursery, these will take several years to mature, but they won't have cost you a penny.

Making grape juice or juice concentrate from fresh backyard grapes is truly easy. Gather your grapes, cutting the clusters with pruning shears or scissors rather than yanking them off the vines. Ripe grapes slip easily from their stems, and trying to yank the clusters will just leave grapes scattered over the ground. Once your grapes are harvested, rinse them, and then roughly stem them—by roughly I mean that, as you pull the grapes from the stems, you will get little pieces of stem still attached to some grapes. This is fine.

Fill quart jars one-third full of whole grapes for juice, or half-full for concentrate. Add no sugar for juice; add one-eighth cup sugar for concentrate. Fill the jars with water, seal, and boil in a water bath for five minutes. Keep the sealed jars in a dark, cool room or cellar until after the New Year for best flavor. Then open, drain the juice into a pitcher, set aside the spent grapes, and serve the juice with ice. For concentrate, add water to taste—I usually add about half as much water, but my wife likes hers to be more tart. Compost the spent grapes, or feed them to your chickens if you have them. At our house we regularly make more than one hundred quarts of grape juice a year. We have pink/red, purple Concord-type, and light green grapes, which are called white grapes. The purple make the sweetest juice. I usually bring up two quarts of juice at a time from the basement cellar, one red or white, the other purple, and mix them for the best taste.

As much as we love the juice, jelly is the favorite grape cellar item at our house. You might be surprised how quickly your homemade grape jelly disappears, or how longingly people recall it if you give it for gifts. ("Longingly recall" is usually a euphemism for broadly hinting that they'd sure like you to give them more!) Half-pint jars of homemade grape jelly make great stocking stuffers. And don't be afraid to make the reduced sugar or no-sugar recipes included in every pectin box. In several dinnertime taste tests, our large family could not tell the difference between

Grape juice bottled fresh from the author's garden (center) surrounded by smaller jars of jelly which will be eaten on waffles, pancakes, sandwiches, and Yorkshire pudding.

reduced sugar and regular-sugar homemade grape jellies, which convinced me to stop making the full-sugar version all together. Not even I could tell the difference. I also make no-sugar jelly using only honey for a sweetener (this recipe also comes inside the pectin box), and believe it or not, the three-year-old sugar addict at our house gobbled it down time after time without noticing any difference. I confess I could tell the difference—the jelly was slightly darker in color (I used dark honey) and not as sweet, but it was still good jelly.

Whether you choose to make full, reduced, or no-sugar jelly—or experiment with all three, like we do at our house—there are countless ways to enjoy this treat. Slathering it on just-from-the-oven homemade wheat bread in the middle of winter goes without saying. Spread it over waffles or pancakes. We eat it on steaming hot Yorkshire pudding, which is our favorite way to use excess homegrown eggs in winter. And, yes, my peanut butter and jelly sandwiches are the best tasting around.

Homegrown grapes can also be eaten straight from the vine, of course. All the varieties we grow at our house are the seeded kind, and the young grandchildren eat them voraciously anyway. (I should note that they are boys, and boys take special joy in spitting seeds, so take this evidence as you may.) I've heard that, like thornless raspberries and blackberries, seedless grapes are less tasty and sugary than their seeded cousins, but I might plant a seedless version anyway one day just for table grapes. Homegrown grapes, seeded or otherwise, can also be "preserved" fresh for a month or two for later eating by placing them in a box in the cellar in single layers, or by hanging them.

I'm also partial to grapes for another reason. They make the perfect edible, zero-maintenance privacy screen if you love your neighbors but don't always want to feel like your backyard is a fish bowl.

I was sitting once in a lecture by a certified Advanced Master gardener who said that homeowners should avoid growing grapes on chain-link fence at all costs. I have to strongly disagree with this advice. The speaker said the grapes would twist the fencing and make a mess. Some of the grapes at our house have lived on a chain link fence for many years without damaging the fence at all. Better yet, the fence is hidden by the vines all summer and fall. The curtain of green is so thick that we take family portraits in front of it. I will confess that our grapes have from time to time grown vines that

> ### Pioneer Stories
>
> In her memoirs, my great-grandmother, Lexia Dastrup Warnock, 1890–1985, recalled the value of their home orchard. "We had a few fruit trees and we waited very impatiently for the 'Early Joe' apples to begin to ripen. We played games of our own manufacture in the black currant bushes, and picked gooseberries and greengages for canning for winter, but the nicest of all were the early apples."

leave the fence and climb all the way to the top of our very tall apple trees. Some people might not be pleased by this, but I thought it was great fun to look at—almost sculptural.

FRUIT TREES

If you've never been, you should plan a family trip this fall to Capitol Reef National Park in central Utah. Once upon a time there was a pioneer outpost town here called Fruita, so named because between the skyscraping red rock cliffs the pioneers planted fruit orchards, which the National Park Service maintains today. The town is long gone, but each autumn the orchards are opened to the public for you-pick harvesting. Visitors pay by the pound for peaches, pears, grapes, apricots, apples, and more in season. Our family has been here many times, and I don't think we've ever *not* seen at least one or two white-tailed deer resting in the orchard shade. The leafy-green trees laden with bright fruit are stunning, set against the red-rock backdrop, and you can visit the original Fruita one-room schoolhouse if you want to take a step back in time. Not to mention that just up the road is a natural waterslide area adjacent to the highway, and camping near the orchards—all in all a great weekend getaway. So great, in fact, that I'm almost reluctant to mention it in this book for fear that more people will find out about it.

Beyond the beauty, there is another reason to visit Fruita, and that is to experience what fruit tasted like *before* the industrial-era fruit tree was born. The taste of the fruit from these old trees is something special. If you've ever tasted a canned peach from the grocery store and compared it to the taste of a sun-ripened peach from a pioneer-era tree, then you know what I'm talking about. Comparison is impossible. The texture of the shipped fruit is fibrous and mealy while the fresh fruit is—well, you know what it is. Fantastic. One of life's true pleasures.

Many pioneer varieties of fruit trees are no longer in production. Not all the trees in Fruita are pioneer stock. The Park Service has added modern varieties over the years. For the true pioneer taste, ask a ranger to point you to the antique trees in the valley.

Tree fruit today mostly arrives in our homes from grocery stores. Even in central Utah you can get *local* apples year-round. This is because the apples are picked and then stored in carbon-dioxide cold-cellars until the off-season market, when growers can get higher prices for them. I've toured these carbon dioxide storage chambers, and they have a place. But this kind of fruit does not taste the same. They have been waxed to help stop the fruit from losing moisture and to keep them shiny for grocery store shelves. They are often crisp and fresh tasting, but the flavor is nothing like the fruit that comes from the now very old pioneer trees.

Many of the pioneer varieties have been abandoned for the same reasons that the vegetables of a century ago are now extinct—they don't lend themselves to cross-country shipping or long-term storage. They bruise easily, they split, they ripen too fast, they go soft too rapidly—any of these are reasons why the commercial growers can't use them to ship to grocery stores nationwide. But none of these are concerns for the backyard grower, and as with open-pollinated seed, a volunteer effort to save historic fruit tree varieties has slowly developed.

Beyond the taste, the historic varieties, which you can't get anywhere else (even local fruit stands have to pick their fruit slightly on the unripe side so they don't spoil or bruise), there are other reasons to have a home orchard. Low-sugar oven-baked jams are a winter pleasure at our house, in both the peach and apricot varieties—as I write this, my wife made more than a gallon of apricot jam today. The flowers on orchard trees are a sight to behold, one of the sure signs that winter is passing into spring. And even unfertilized, benignly neglected fruit trees will produce fruit for many years, though pruning increases both the size of the fruit and the yield of the tree. Pruning also provides free campfire wood. And a place for backyard tree houses.

There are some fruit tree companies that have worked to bring back some of the old pioneer varieties that had dropped off the market. All are surely worth saving for the taste of the fruit alone. Some are better suited to micro-climates, producing fruit earlier or later than the commercial standards. Some process more easily for canning, some resist frost better, some are best for pies, some offer colors other than the norm, or tartness, or better long-term storage in the cellar. I have stored apples from some of our trees in our root cellar into February, for example. Others have reported success in storing apples by placing them in a bucket with dry ice, which forces out corroding oxygen and preserves the fruit using basically the same method employed by commercial growers.

An apple ripe for the picking. All fruits and vegetables in the author's garden are organically grown. Backyard apples make for a quick Sunday apple pie or fresh apple juice.

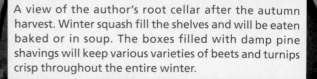

A view of the author's root cellar after the autumn harvest. Winter squash fill the shelves and will be eaten baked or in soup. The boxes filled with damp pine shavings will keep various varieties of beets and turnips crisp throughout the entire winter.

ORCHARDS

645 So Alpine Hwy.
Alpine, Utah 84004
UDAF 0-50

20 LBS. NET

CHAPTER 10

SIMPLE PIONEER CELLARING SOLUTIONS

Many traditional cellaring methods are not only simple and practical but also exceedingly affordable. Families with self-reliance in mind will find that the following cellaring methods require no extra electricity, no expensive construction, and little maintenance while allowing self-sufficient, long-term storage of wholesome homegrown food. For families looking to extend the home garden harvest across the calendar, cellars are often as important as the garden itself.

STRAW-CELLARING

Following in the footsteps of the settlers, savvy modern gardeners can store their carrots, onions, and parsnips over winter by leaving them exactly where they grew in the garden. Simply spread a thick layer of straw over these vegetables, about a foot and a half to two feet deep. I do this just before or just after the first hard frost of the fall. The straw should be one continuous large blanket for best results, though I have had success placing chunks of straw over scattered individual onions.

Where I live, we have below-zero winter temperatures, and it is not unusual to go four or five weeks in a row without the temperature ever rising above freezing. Through all of this, however, the ground in my garden never froze under the straw "blanket," and I was able to easily dig carrots, even under two feet of snow. Using a regular garden shovel, I scooped the snow away, carefully lifted up a section of straw, dug up the carrots, replaced the straw, and then scooped the snow back over the straw. This last step is important because snow over straw acts as a blanket of its own, helping to insulate what's below from the temperature swings above.

When you move the straw to dig out your carrots or parsnips, the green tops have long since died back. Any bit of carrot sticking out above the soil will have gone soft, but anything below the soil will be fresh, crisp, and sweet. Simply dig them up, trim the tops, and eat. Because no one really loves to dig carrots in two feet of snow, I wait until a day with a bit of afternoon sun. Taking a large bowl or box into the garden, I remove the snow, lift the straw, and dig dozens of carrots. After replacing the layers of straw and snow, I rinse the carrots but don't trim them. Then I put them in the fridge in a plastic bag, where they stay fresh, crisp, and easily accessible for a month.

I first learned about this straw-cellaring method when I happened to visit a neighbor in January. The woman of the house came in from the snow-covered garden with a clutch of just-dug carrots in her hand. I was astounded. Where had they come from? The homeowners explained that in autumn they had gathered fallen leaves into plastic kitchen garbage sacks and laid these pillows of leaves directly over the carrot rows. Whenever they wanted fresh winter carrots, they lifted up the bag, dug the carrots, and replaced the bag of leaves. I was excited to try this discovery, but when I mentioned it to a few other old-timer gardeners, they told me that straw works just as well and does not need to be stuffed into trash bags. So I've never used bags of leaves in my garden, but I've seen it work. Take your pick.

Where we live we have terrible winter windstorms, strong enough to rip huge sections of shingles off the roof of the house and barn. Winds up to 100 mph are not uncommon. I was afraid that the straw would be blown everywhere, but I needn't have worried. Occasional autumn rains keep the straw heavy, and then the straw is covered with snow. I mulch my garden with layers of leaves, both my own leaves and any I can get from neighbors. To keep the leaves from blowing everywhere I have to lay old boards over them, but I've never had any trouble with my straw blowing, and I've never had to lay boards or anything over the straw.

Another great benefit of straw-cellaring directly in the garden is that the thick straw keeps out the weeds. I leave the straw on the garden until just before I want to plant in May. While weeds are a foot high in the bare garden, wherever there is a blanket of straw, there are no weeds.

To move the straw I lay a tarp on the ground, rake the straw onto the tarp, and drag the straw to where it's needed next. Then I'm ready to plant the garden. I recycle the straw into the potato grow-boxes (more on that in another chapter) or put the straw between garden rows or on paths to keep down weeds, or pile it somewhere out of the way in the pasture for our free-range chickens to root through—and they love it. I also till straw directly into the spring soil. It makes a great soil amendment.

I have not grown salsify or Jerusalem artichokes, but Mike and Nancy Bubel in their book *Root Cellaring* report that straw-cellaring, which they call garden-row storage, works with these too. They report some success with turnips, and occasional problems with mice eating some of the vegetables left under the straw. We have lots of winter mice in our barn, but we've never had a problem with them eating vegetables under the straw. The Bubels

Corn growing up through straw-covered ground. Straw and leaves help keep weeds out of the garden, allowing the gardener to focus on more important summer tasks—like eating the garden's bounty!

suggest placing a layer of window screening, sold inexpensively in rolls at any hardware store, over the vegetables before layering down the straw to solve the mouse problem.

STRAW-BOX CELLARING

When I was a child, our family would dig potatoes from the LDS stake farm and take them home in enormous bags. We'd take these potatoes out to a corner of sage brush-covered land bordering our family farm and build a "box" from straw bales to keep them in. Anytime we ran short of potatoes at the house during winter, my father and I would drive out through the snow with the truck, remove the top straw bales, pull out a bag of potatoes, still firm and crisp and never frozen, and take them home.

To use this great old method, build a tight four-walled box using straw bales stacked two-high. Place potatoes or any other root vegetables inside, and cover with tightly placed straw bales.

At my house today I keep 50-pound bags (they come in paper bags these days instead of burlap) of unwashed, dirt-on, huge Idaho potatoes in our root cellar and move one bag at a time into the garage for easy access as winter wears on. I buy these potatoes in late September, and whatever I have left in June I use to plant in the garden. This method works well for us because we have a root cellar, but the straw-box cellar would work just as well for any family without a root cellar.

In their book *Root Cellaring*, the Bubels say that building individual straw boxes around a small cluster or single plant of lettuce, tomato, chard, or broccoli before the first freeze prolongs the harvest of these up to a month. I haven't tried this, but it may be worth experimenting with if you are just not in the mood to give up your tomatoes.

DUG-OUT CELLARING

To keep dirt-on potatoes crisp and firm the entire winter without a root cellar, dig a hole in the garden at least four feet deep, but small enough around to be completely covered by straw bales. Transfer bags of potatoes from this hole to the garage as needed during winter.

GARAGE-CELLARING:

Anyone with an unheated garage can easily use this space for long-term storage of dirt-on potatoes, hanging corn, hanging tomatoes, winter squash, grapes, and much more. Here is a guide to garage-cellaring and storage:

Potatoes

Store potatoes away from light and heat. If your garage door is often open, your potatoes must be in a dark box with small holes for air flow. A box made of untreated wood is ideal. No vegetable should ever be in contact with concrete. Concrete quickly sucks moisture from vegetables, causing rapid spoilage.

Straw bales can be used to create an inexpensive outdoor cellar for overwintering garden vegetables.

Potatoes are best kept on wooden planks or shelves. Garage-cellared potatoes at our house have remained solid and crisp for up to five months.

Carrots, Parsnips, Turnips, Rutabaga, Beets, & Winter-type Radishes

Leave the dirt on, and trim tops to one inch. Layer in a sturdy cardboard or wooden box with damp sand, sawdust, pine shavings, or peat moss, leaving an inch between layers. For best storage, no vegetable should touch another. If kept damp, cool, and out of light completely, long-keeper varieties will keep several months in the garage using this method.

Cabbage

Crisp, long-keeper varieties will store in the garage on wood planks or shelves, but may make your garage smell sulfurous over time. Cabbage will do better if kept in the dark and stored on top of wet sand, sawdust, pine shavings, or peat moss. If you are like us and don't expect to use too many heads of cabbage over the winter, I've found the best solution is simply to peel off the outer leaves, rinse the cabbages, and keep them in the fridge vegetable drawer, cutting slices off as wanted.

Onions

Onions are finicky to store. They demand a lot of air circulation, or they will go soft. They can be kept in the garage or a basement storage room in a single layer on cardboard or wood shelving for two to three months; no onion is allowed to touch another. They will last longer if hung in a dark place in a net bag or wire vegetable basket.

Some growers speaking lovingly of braiding onions and hanging them in their kitchen or storage room, but every time I've tried this, the braid has either fallen apart on the spot, or I go into the storage room a week later to find the onions on the floor. Maybe you'll have better luck. Keep in mind that onions should be cured in direct sunlight for several days before being placed into storage. And if you plan to store onions, you must grow storage-type onions. I learned the hard way one year that walla-wallas don't store well at all.

SO YOU WANT TO BUILD A ROOT CELLAR . . .

The Bubels present a detailed list of root cellar designs in *Root Cellaring*, with instructions for construction and diagrams.

VEGETABLES THAT NEED NO CELLARING

As mentioned in chapter six, certain cold-hardy vegetable varieties can be left in the garden all winter, exactly where they grew. These require no cellaring at all.

This salad was picked fresh from the author's garden on January 16, 2011, and was grown without electricity or artificial heat of any kind.

Here are some heirloom varieties of perishable vegetables that are prized for storing surprisingly well:

STOWELL'S EVERGREEN SWEET CORN

This corn was traditionally hung, stalk and all, in cellars by homesteaders to be enjoyed far into the winter season. Seed Savers Exchange members report this corn was introduced in 1848 by Nathan Stowell. According to the Baker Creek Heirloom Seeds 2010 catalog, this corn "is among the oldest sweet corn that is still in production, predating 1949." That description alone speaks volumes about how much we as a nation of gardeners and farmers have now come to rely on hybrid seed. "It is still a favorite of many, producing tasty white kernels. The plants used to be pulled up when completely ripe, and hung upside-down in a cool pantry; the ears would last well into the winter in a semi-fresh state. In 1873, the seeds sold for 25 cents per pint."[1]

I grew this corn for the first time in 2010, and as I write this in mid-October the stalks are hanging in my garage. And they taste great.

Stowell's Evergreen Sweet Corn hanging upside down in the author's garage. This 1848 sweet corn is believed to be among the oldest sweet corn still in production today. This corn was stored for winter eating by the pioneers. In the author's garage the corn stayed fresh and sweet for ten weeks.

REVEREND MORROW'S LONG KEEPER TOMATO

I'm a strange gardener when it comes to tomatoes. I don't like them. Several members of my family are oddly allergic to fresh tomatoes. I crave the smell of tomato plants, however. Before I was married I used to grow them just to smell the plants—I gave away all the tomatoes. I'm not an expert at tomatoes, but my wife loves tomatoes and mourns their passing with the first frost above everything else in the garden. We pay close attention to the weather and gather in all the green tomatoes (not the small white ones, which are too young to be of use) the evening before the first frost. She lays them in a box in a single layer on newspaper, where they slowly ripen in the warm house. She does this with whatever varieties of tomato we are growing that year, and we can always extend the harvest a few weeks, sometimes even into October, and once into November. Tomato plants can also be pulled whole from the garden and hung upside down in the garage or cellar. Harvest the tomatoes as they ripen.

I have tried, in my annual seed search, to find any catalog that lists tomatoes in a long-keeper category, but I have yet to stumble upon one. Even Seed Savers Exchange does not group tomatoes or any other vegetables by their ability for excellent storage. In the fall of 2009, I stumbled upon Reverend Morrow's Long Keeper in the Baker Creek Heirloom Seeds catalog. They describe this variety this way: "The amazing thing about this tomato is its keeping qualities; these have kept until January! Selected for longest storage time possible, by Merl Neidens. Plant late for storage use, and keep cool in storage."[2] These tomatoes are growing in my garden now. As with the hanging corn, a full report will be posted on my blog at CalebWarnock.blogspot.com.

Among the 4,639 varieties of tomatoes offered in 2010 by Seed Savers Exchange members, the following are mentioned as having long-keeper traits:

- Hopkins Stewart Longkeeper, a yellow cherry tomato.
- Mercuri Winter Keeper, yellow-orange, lasts to December, occasionally into summer.
- Graham's Good Keeper, an early red tomato that also keeps well

- Reverend Morrow's Peach, late maturing, shelf-ripening tomato
- Long-Keeper, Burpee's, red/pink tomato that stores for months
- Winterkeeper, pale yellow skin, red flesh long keeper.

RAMPICANTE (ITALIAN VINING ZUCCHINI)

This is one of my all-time most-loved garden vegetables because it does double duty as both a summer zucchini and a winter butternut-type squash. This Italian heirloom is a vining summer squash rather than a bush plant. The fruit is long and trumpet-shaped, curls gently, and features medium

Rampicante Italian Vining Zucchini is among my favorite of all vegetables, and is almost unheard of in America—which is a shame. This beautiful zucchini tastes sweeter than any other zucchini, but best of all, the fruit becomes a winter squash with a butternut taste when left to mature in the garden. And all the seeds are contained in a single bulb at the bottom of the fruit.

to light-green striped skin. The flesh looks like other zucchini but tastes sweeter, another reason this squash should be more popular. All the seeds are contained in a small bulb at the end of the long fruit, so this zucchini is easy to use and does not need to be picked within days of appearing on the vine to be tender and tasty, as other summer squash does.

If left to mature on the vine, rampicante stores excellently through winter, developing a butternut taste and texture. In storage and even late in the garden, rampicante slowly fades to a pale butter color. We use this winter squash in the crock pot with a roast, raw in salad, in many soups, with oven-roasted vegetables, or sautéed.

Like rampicante, certain other normally perishable vegetables are available in varieties traditionally kept in the cellar, some through Christmas and beyond. Seed Savers Exchange members offer the following:

WINTER-TYPE RADISHES

Agata
Arbuznaya
Black Soviet
Black Spanish Round
Black Winter Round
Blauer Herbst Und Winter
China Rose
Chinese Green Meat
Cylindra
Daikon Gostinets
Daikon Sasha
Dziunaya
Madras Podding
Slobolt
Weiner Runder Kohlschwarzer

LONG-KEEPER BEETS

Bordo 237
Deacon Dan's
Detroit Dark Red

Dvukhsemyannaya Tsha (yes, that's the actual name)
Early Blood Turnip Rooted (yes, it's actually a beet)
Feuer Kugel
Forono
Lutz Green Leaf
Lutz Winter Keeper
Sweetheart

LONG-KEEPER WATERMELONS

Blacktail Mountain (keeps six weeks)
Citron Red Seeded (very long keeper, for preserves, not edible raw)
Crimson Sweet
Kholodok (stores 3–5 months)
Nambe Yellow

LONG-KEEPER MELONS

Casaba Golden Beauty
Collective Farm Woman
Golden Honeymoon
Lada
Zoloistaja
Altaiskaya
Banana
Schoon's Hardshell
Vert Grimpant

Notes

1. Baker Creek Heirloom seeds, "Stowell's Evergreen Sweet Corn."
2. Ibid., "Rev. Morrow's Long Keeper."

The pioneers who settled the West and generations of families throughout time who simply wanted to fend off the hunger gap developed and made use of *early-season* vegetables as a way of jump-starting the growing season.

Most, if not all, vegetables can be found in early varieties. Some of the heritage seed offered by Seed Savers Exchange boasts extremely early traits, sometimes cutting normal growth times in half—including an extraordinary 40-day tomato, and an astonishing number of tomato plants that take *fifty-nine* days or less to mature. Such quick-growing varieties are invaluable for shrinking the wait required from planting to eating. The loss of these varieties would greatly reduce our ability to extend the harvest season backward into the hunger gap.

In my garden, the earliest varieties are often the only thing standing between a vegetable crop and no crop. We live in a mountain bench community in central Utah, where we "enjoy" the shortest growing season in the county—ninety-two days, according to the Utah State University Extension Service. But even for gardeners with a much longer season, short-season vegetables offer a natural way to enjoy wholesome, fresh-picked produce longer.

Early and late vegetable types are not the only reason to keep open-pollinated seed around. Many such seeds were developed over generations for niche climates, making them exceptional growers where other vegetables struggle. And they offer a glimpse of how much more is possible than what we see on grocery store shelves—myriad colors and color combinations, shapes, sizes, flavors, and uses.

Working to save what is left of seed lines abandoned by commercial growers, Exchange members often offer more choices than vendors, sometimes far more choices. The Exchange organization tracks all of this, compiling each year a publication called the *Garden Seed Inventory*, which lists every commercial seller of non-hybrid seed and the varieties they offer. Using these resources, Suzanne Ashworth in *Seed to Seed* reports that Exchange members offer:

- 88 varieties of multiplying onions; commercial vendors offer 38.
- 50 varieties of rutabaga; vendors offer 26
- 11 collards versus 4 from vendors
- 101 Jerusalem artichokes versus 12 from vendors
- 1,413 common beans versus 704 from vendors
- 719 peas versus 230 from vendors.[1]

This list is just a sample of the data available. In other cases, members list about the same number as vendors, and in some cases, vendors list more. Because members are private gardeners, not every variety is listed every year.

In the information below, each vegetable is listed by a number of days, counted from the appearance of the plant's first true leaves to the day of the first mature fruit. This count generally does not include the number of days it took from planting to sprouting. To compile this list, I took the earliest recorded day-count listed by any Exchange member. Exchange members growing the same variety sometimes agree on the day-count, and sometimes they do not. This is because nurture affects the growth of plants as much as genetic nature. For example, the Jaune Flamme Orange tomato is listed by one Exchange member as a 55-day tomato, but another member lists it as a 60-day tomato, and other members lists it as an even longer-day variety. The day-count numbers below should be taken as a guide, not a guarantee. Experiment in your area to see which of the earliest of the early vegetables thrive for you.

THE EARLIEST VEGETABLE VARIETIES (DATA FROM SEED SAVERS EXCHANGE)

18-day radishes (aptly named 18 Days)
20-day radishes (Malaga, Mokhovsky, Smachny, Yuki Komaki Hatsuka, Zhara)

A green-black skinned "Noir des Carmes" cantaloupe is the author's favorite melon to grow, for three reasons: the melon matures in a mere 65 days, making it one of the earliest of all melons; it produces prolifically all season; and the whole melon turns orange overnight when the fruit is ready to eat, so you always know when these are ripe!

Making Sugar from Garden Beets

I was recently reminded that in his book *The Self-sufficient Life and How to Live It*, John Seymour gives brief instructions for producing sugar at home from sugar beets. Sugar beet seed has become difficult to find, especially seed that is open pollinated. (Mangels, a type of beet that was routinely feed to farm animals in winter, have also become difficult to find seed for.) I happened to have a few Albino beets growing in my garden, an heirloom variety of sugar beet from Holland offered by Baker Creek Heirloom Seeds. So I pulled up a couple and give sugar-making a whirl.

Beet sugar is made by extracting the juice, and then reducing the juice to sugar. Seymour suggests juicing the beets by using a car jack or cider press. Our cider press is missing a part, and the car jack idea didn't sound very sanitary. Instead, I opted to finely grate the beets, using a granite pestle to press the juice through a fine-mesh strainer. From two beets I got about two tablespoons of juice. The Albino beet is a pure white variety that I grow because when cooked it has a supremely sugary flavor. This flavor is almost perfectly retained when the beets are blanched and frozen, and I enjoy eating these sugar beets in the middle of winter. Interestingly, the white pulp began to oxide almost immediately as I grated it, quickly turning brown much like apples being ground for juice. The juice itself turned white to brown to a creamy black in less than a minute.

I took this admittedly scant bit of juice and boiled it, per Seymour's instructions, to remove the water and leave the sugars. This happened very quickly, so quickly in fact, that I believe I caramelized the sugar. What I got in the end was about a quarter-teaspoon of thick and sticky black beet sugar that looked and smelled like molasses. Four of us tasted it, and all agreed the flavor was of overcooked-caramel and molasses, with a beety-vegetable aftertaste that became stronger after a minute or two had passed. I think we all required a drink of water afterward. For the sake of information, I'll mention that I boiled the juice on medium-high heat in a ceramic-coated nonstick pan, stirring with a silicone spatula.

When my remaining sugar beets are a bit larger—they are golf ball-sized now—I'll probably try this experiment again, this time evaporating the water out of the juice on very low heat, rather than by boiling. Boil was the term Seymour uses in his instructions (p. 384), and perhaps that may work with a larger quantity of juice. I'm sure he didn't foresee someone attempting the whole thing on a whim with the juice of just two small beets. It was fun to try and fun to taste, however, and you may enjoy attempting beet sugar at home if you can get a hold of some sugar beet seed. The Albino beet variety is worth growing just for the taste, at any rate.

Turnips and beets on a pine-plank table, ready for eating. The two turnips in the center, both "Boule d'Or" are the author's favorite type of turnip because they are so sweet and lack the tang of the common turnip.

30-day lettuce (Parris Island Cos)
30-day Swiss chard (Kiwi Green)
30-day spinach (Erste Ernte, Zhirnolistnyi)
30-day green onions (He-Shi-Ko Bunching, Russkiy Zimniy)
35-day hot peppers (Flame Tongue)
35-day cucumbers (Korall)
36-day summer squash (Beloplodnyi)
40-day tomato (Vee One)
40-day turnips (Shogoin, Snowball)
45-day kale (Frizee, Oregreen Curled)
55-day corn (Bear Island Flint)

60-day eggplants (Patsekha, Snowy)
60-day watermelon (Bozeman)
65-day melons (Collective Farm Woman, Sweet Granite)
65-day globe onion (Karmen)
84-day leeks (King Sieg)

Note

1. Ashworth, *Seed to Seed,* 41, 49, 54, 88, 136, 137.

Utah Sugar Beets

In her memoirs, my great-grandmother, Lexia Dastrup Warnock, 1890–1985, recalled working on the family sugar beet farm. "They began raising sugar beets here when I was a kid. The planting was done with machine. When the beets were two inches high it was time to thin them to one beet in a place. Each kid then had a 4-inch-wide hoe with a short handle, we cut out the four inch piece of row, thinned to one beet, made another cut, and repeated the process. We children crawled up the rows leaving the row clean of weeds and trying to leave single beets in each place. We were paid about five cents a hundred yards. . . . In autumn came the beet harvest. The beets were plowed loose. Then the men with big beet knives with a hook on the end went to work. With the knife they hooked the beet out, grasped it firmly with one hand, chopped its top off, and threw the beets in a pile. Other men came with the beet wagon and forks and pitched the beets on the wagon. They were hauled to the beet dump, weighed, tested, and unloaded in a railroad car and hauled to the factory. Raising beets was hard work, and work for everybody."

Tips for Storing Seed

For year-to-year storage, keep your self-sufficient seed in paper envelopes in a cool, dry, dark place securely out of reach from pests or vermin.

For long-term storage, keep seed in the freezer in clearly labeled freezer bags.

Some seed needs no collection or storage at all. Open-pollinated lettuce will self-seed to come up the next year if not tilled under. The same with cosmos flowers.

CHAPTER 13

PIONEER YEAST

Pioneer yeast, also called wild yeast, homemade yeast, or natural yeast, was the sole method for raising bread for more than 6,000 years, before the invention of increasingly suspect rapid-rise and quick-rise yeasts.

There have been uncovered in Egypt massive bread bakeries that were used to feed the workers who built the pyramids and other iconic ancient structures. We know from the Bible and many other sources that bread has long been a staple food all over the world. But few of us today could manage to make mass quantities of daily bread the way the Egyptians did without turning to a store for bulk yeast. The Egyptians did not have yeast sealed in foil packets or jars, nor did the pilgrims or pioneers—there were certainly no yeast vendors strung along the handcart trail leading West and no supermarkets waiting with supplies along the handcart trail.

So how did the pioneers, pilgrims, Egyptians, Israelites, and everyone else get yeast?

The answer is simple. From family and community, and originally, from the air.

The everyday use of pioneer yeast is one of those skills that has nearly vanished from the general population but deserves new consideration. Pioneer yeast is sometimes called wild yeast and often called sourdough starter, even though it is not always sour. Pioneer yeast is simple to use, costs nothing, tastes wonderful, completely cuts out the need to buy commercial yeast, and drastically reduces the need for baking powder and baking soda. I use pioneer yeast not only to make bread, but also waffles, pancakes, breadsticks, pizza dough, scones, rolls, and even old-fashioned root beer.

My yeast "start," as they are called, came from a friend, who herself had gotten it from a friend, who had gotten it from LDShealth.ning.com, which sells starters for a $5 mail-order and claims theirs comes from a family line nearly two hundred years old. It's been a wonderful yeast for me.

Beyond flavor, price, and the self-sufficiency this yeast allows, there may be another reason to use it. Both the LDS Health website and other sources claim that using this kind of slower-rising yeast is better for our health because it pre-digests the glutens in wheat flour better. James and Colleen Simmons, authors of *Daniel's Challenge* and *Original Fast Foods*, and owners of LDShealth.ning.com, have this to say on the subject:

> "The commercial bread-making industry figured out how to isolate strains of yeast that made bread raise very quickly compared to the old-fashion bread-making method; soon sourdough starts became a thing of the past for most of us. What we didn't know when we traded Old-World leavening techniques for quick-rise yeasts, is that not everything in wheat is good for you. In fact, there are several elements in wheat that are down-right problematic and that have led to grain intolerances in about 20 percent of today's population. When you compare what happens to the bread when it is leavened with commercial yeasts versus a good sourdough starter, another story unfolds. . . . The sourdough starter contains several natural strains of friendly bacteria and yeasts that also cause bread to rise; however, these friendly bacteria also neutralize the harmful effects of the grain. They neutralize phytic acids that otherwise prevent minerals found in the grain from being absorbed properly; they predigest the gluten, and they also neutralize lignans and tanins found in wheat."[1]

Proving or disproving these claims is beyond the scope and intent of this book, and I will leave it to you, the reader, to contemplate the merits of rapid-rise yeast versus pioneer yeast.

Caring for pioneer yeast is both simple and enjoyable. Pioneers kept theirs in crocks with lids; I keep mine in glass canning jars. Yeast is a living organism and was likely the first domesticated living creature on earth. Yeast fungi feed on natural starch and sugars in grains and convert them into carbon dioxide bubbles, which leaven. In fact, the word *yeast* is said to come from the Old English word *gyst*, which means foam or bubble. A minute amount of alcohol is also naturally produced as yeast digests starch and sugar; this is burned away when the dough is baked.

KEEPING PIONEER YEAST WITHOUT REFRIGERATION

Pioneer technology trumps anything modern, in this case. The advantage of room-temperature yeast is this: it is available for immediate use, with little or no planning ahead required. In our busy household, this is a wonderful advantage. I can make yeast-raised waffles or pancakes at a moment's notice or have bread dough ready to rise in fifteen minutes. The flavor of room-temperature yeast is unmatched, with a nutty, earthy tang that lends itself especially well to waffles and pancakes—delicious! Topped with butter or homemade jam or jelly, this is a breakfast (or lunch) that can't be beat. For instant homemade waffles to use another day, I double the waffle batter, cook up the extra, and put them in the freezer.

Pioneer yeast is a wet doughy mix, not a powder. The pioneers used homemade dry yeast too (more on

Oatmeal waffles made using pioneer yeast take only minutes to prepare and taste delicious.

that in a minute), but mostly as a long-term storage backup. In the directions below, the word yeast describes a wet mix, the consistency of pancake batter.

To use pioneer yeast, you'll need a start. It is possible to start yeast from the air in your kitchen, and you can find directions for this all over the Internet, if you are interested, but it's easier to get a start from someone else.

After living with them for years, even decades, people tend to think of their yeast starters as members of the family. If you don't know anyone with a start, ask around in your family, ward, and stake, or purchase a start from a reputable source on the Internet or at a local health food store, or ask for one on your local Freecycle group (more on them in a later chapter). When giving starts away, or dividing a start for my own backup, I always use a sterile jar and lid, with food safety in mind.

A start is kept alive by feeding it wheat flour. Flour and water should be added to the yeast jar in equal amounts. I usually use whole wheat flour that I've ground myself, but any store-bought flour will do.

After it is fed, yeast rises. There are three options for allowing yeast to rise:

- At room temperature, the peak rise will take two to three hours, and begin to develop a sour dough flavor. Some yeast strains develop little or no sour dough flavor, but most will slowly become tangy at room temperature.
- If placed immediately in the fridge after feeding, the start will rise much slower, and may take as long as week to achieve peak rise. Chilled starts also develop a lesser sour-dough flavor.
- In a combination approach, feed the start and allow to achieve peak rise at room temperature. Then place in the fridge, where it will often stay at peak rise for up to a day. If you know you want to make pioneer yeast waffles in the morning, feeding a start the night before, allowing it to achieve peak rise, and then placing it in the fridge overnight mean the start can be immediately used in the morning. (In pioneer waffle and pancake recipes, no flour is added. The start provides the flour, much of the moisture, and the leavening.)

A half-quart of just-fed starter will become nearly a full quart at peak rise, so plan accordingly. Starter should always be allowed to rise in a lidded jar.

When you are ready to cook or bake, measure out the amount of starter called for in the recipe. For bread, two cups is equal to a tablespoon of dry yeast, or one store-bought packet. Three cups of pioneer yeast, the equivalent of one and a half tablespoons of dry yeast, is usually what is needed to make a batch of bread requiring seven cups of flour. Using this much yeast will typically take most of your start if you are keeping it in a quart jar. Never fear, however, because just the remnant on the sides of the jar, rejuvenated with water and flour added in equal parts, is enough to leaven a new batch of pioneer yeast.

Several people have told me that room-temperature yeast must be "fed" flour and water every day or it will die. I have not found this to be true. I've neglected mine up to a week, and regularly leave it unfed for three and four days at a time, especially on hot summer days when I'm in no hurry to turn on the stove or oven. This benign neglect has worked well for me. A layer of harmless liquid rises to the top over time, clear at first, and turning dark over several days. I pour this liquid off before using the yeast. Most people say refrigerated wild yeast needs to be fed once a week, but I've let mine go up to two weeks without any problems. Because pioneer yeast is a living microorganism, it can die. You may forget to feed it for too long, or it may develop an off-color within the yeast batter (not the liquid that may rise to the top). If this happens, throw the entire starter away. I always keep one start in the fridge and second on the counter.

FREEZING PIONEER YEAST

Frozen starter is a back-up, in case your active starter should fail or die. To freeze a start, take a portion of yeast at peak rise, put it in a plastic freezer bag, or a glass jar, and place it in the freezer. While I've heard of yeast keeping for years this way, replacing the frozen starter once a year is probably a good guideline. To use, bring to room temperature, and then feed to activate.

DRYING PIONEER YEAST

The advantage of dry yeast, both today and in the pioneer era, is that if your wet yeast dies, you have a backup. Dry yeast keeps many years, if not indefinitely.

To dry yeast, spread a very thin layer on a cookie sheet or wax paper and let it air dry on a window sill or in direct sunlight, taking care not to expose it to insects. You can also warm an oven to its lowest setting, turn the oven off, and then put the thinly layered yeast in the oven to dry. Once thoroughly dried, scrape the flakes and store in a cool, dark place in a sealed container.

Note

1. "Making a Healthful Use of Stored Wheat," LDShealth.ning.com.

CHAPTER 14

MODERN IDEAS THE PIONEERS WOULD HAVE APPRECIATED

FREECYCLE.ORG

This is an free, Internet-based nonprofit group focused on helping people help themselves by giving away things they don't need to people who can use them. There are no fees. People give away anything and everything on this site, and no one is charged a cent for any of it. You can even float a request for a needed or desired item to see if someone in your area has that item to give away. Some of the items I've seen given away over the past several years of particularly of interest to families focused on provident and self-sufficient living include:

- Fresh garden vegetables
- You-pick fruit from home orchards
- Canning jars
- Garden seed
- Lumber
- Hay bales, straw bales
- Chicken feed, storage grains, dried beans
- Laying hens and roosters
- Pet food and supplies
- You-dig raspberry plants, strawberries, blackberries, rhubarb, and so on.
- Fencing supplies
- Canned food

- Children's clothes, toys, books, strollers, and much more.
- Working washing machines, dryers, fridges, freezers
- Pianos
- Furniture
- Lawn mowers, trimmers, garden tools, power tools

The service is organized geographically, grouping nearby people. In our county, there are three Freecycle groups, one covering the north end of the county, another for the south, and a third for the central area. This site is also a great way to find a good home for usable objects that are taking up space in your closets, garage, or basement.

ETSY.COM

More and more people, especially stay-at-home mothers, are earning income and even building businesses by selling their unique handmade items, both to the world via the Internet and in local event-boutiques. Etsy.com has become the global market place for people looking to buy or sell handcrafted item ranging from quilts to clothes, jewelry, bags and purses, art, games, craft kits, holiday decorations, themed items, and much more. Truly old crafts are finding new life through these venues, including:

- Bookplate making
- Origami (paper folding)
- Papermaking
- Leather carving
- Copper-foil stained glass design
- Tatting (handcrafted lace)
- Pattern making
- Terrariums and hanging gardens
- Candy-making
- Fretwork (interlaced carving or metalwork)
- Inlay
- Knife-making

In addition to online sales, there has also been an increasingly successful event-boutique business. These boutiques are often held around Mother's Day and Christmas and feature a select number of displays from local handicraft artists. These boutiques often get three times more applications for space than space available; the more unique an item is, the more likely organizers are to choose it. These events offer another way for local artisans and crafters to find buyers for their wares.

FREESALES

A kind of inverse yard sale, people put usable items out on their lawn for free to anyone who will haul them away. This is usually done on a Friday or Saturday morning, during the traditional yard sale times, but as this idea has spread, more weekday freesales have begun to appear. People give away furniture, clothes, household items, bicycles, toys, exercise equipment, books, appliances—anything they think someone might be willing to haul away and use. The point of this is to simply reduce clutter or find a home for good items that are not now being used. There is no organization to join. Freesales are simply held at will.

SMALL SEED EXCHANGES

This is a truly exciting trend for any gardener. Several counties along the Wasatch Front in Utah now have free annual seed exchanges, often hosted by the local Extension Service office, a botanical garden, or a club or organization. Community members are invited to bring leftover or unused garden seed to give away, and browse the offerings for any seed they may want to take home. Garden organizations and certified master gardeners are often present with information and to answer questions. To find a seed exchange event in your area, call your county office of the Utah State University Extension Service.

WARD, STAKE, AND COMMUNITY GARDENS

Since the collapse of the global economy, there has been a tremendous surge of interest in communal gardens. Many wards and stakes in Utah and around the West are creating group gardens for the first time, often on land owned by local members. The ward works together to till, plant, fertilize, water, weed, and harvest. The produce often goes to families who have lost jobs or are otherwise struggling. I know of one ward, which not only created huge organic garden, but also built a root cellar from which to feed needy member families during the winter. Relief Society members canned hundreds of bottles of fruit and vegetables. In addition to feeding families and individuals struggling to make ends meet, these gardens have fostered new bonds among ward and stake members, taken weedy lots and transformed them into productive land, taught youth and adults new gardening and self-sufficiency skills, and given members an opportunity to demonstrate caring and compassion. Community gardens have accomplished many of the same results while being organized on a smaller scale, often with just a few families participating.

FREE FRUIT AND VEGETABLE STANDS

This is the revival of an old idea: some small communities and neighborhoods once had a certain spot—the corner of someone's yard or a public right of way—where anyone with excess garden vegetables and fruits could simply drop them off at their convenience. Passersby would see something they wanted and take it home with them. The resurgence of this old tradition, like many other changes, seems to be rooted in the economy. Those who have are looking for simple ways to directly but quietly give to those without. This is an idea that any neighborhood, ward, stake, or community could easily adopt.

FARMER'S MARKETS

There has been an explosion in the number of local outdoor markets offering an opportunity for both established and start-up vendors to sell their wares. There are several well-established annual summer markets along the Wasatch Front, and as they became more difficult and expensive for vendors to join, new markets have sprung up. Some struggling historic downtown business areas have seen renewed interest and increased foot traffic after launching a farmers market. These markets are known for being a hub of local produce, honey, eggs, and crafts ranging from jewelry to furniture and art. Markets often feature live music and performances, and some reserve space for humanitarian organizations.

SUBSCRIPTION FARMS

Commonly called CSAs, which stands for Community Supported Agriculture, these ventures are allowing small family farms to thrive again. Community members purchase a "share" in the produce, which is then delivered weekly to certain drop-off points for pickup. Subscription farms usually feature organic produce; some even boast high-tech greenhouses allowing year-round tomatoes and other out-of-season vegetables. In addition to offering fresh food to the public, these farms often partner with local restaurants to supply seasonal produce for the menu. Subscriptions typically run about $15–$20 a week. CSAs often feature family-friendly events on the farm ranging from food and tasting demonstrations, to festivals, to harvesting and even barn-raisings.

COMMUNITY TRADE

Bartering is on the rise, both in person and on the Internet. Several online sites allow people to barter, trading items or services directly without

Pioneer Stories

In her memoirs, my great-grandmother, Lexia Dastrup Warnock, 1890–1985, recalled the pioneer bartering system. "The railroad came through in 1869 but did not reach Sevier Valley until I was six years old in 1896. Until that time my father spent his winters 'freighting' that is, hauling farm produce to the mining camps where he sold it for cash. . . . Trade among the home people was mostly trade—barter—trading my produce or labor for whatever you had to offer. Cash or money was scarce.

"When I was a child, you couldn't go to the store and buy a head of lettuce. They just didn't have any there. They had eggs that they brought from the farmer, and you could buy them from the store or the farmer would sell extra butter that he made. Anything that he wanted to get rid of he'd sell it to the store, or rather, trade it for what the store had that he wanted."

exchanging money. Some sites focus on trading only a narrow range of items—books, for example. Other sites, such as Craigslist.com, allow people in a local area to offer up services or items directly in exchange for other services or items. I know someone who traded a horse for an airline ticket, and another horse for mechanic's services. This type of old-world economy gives cash-strapped but skilled workers an alternative way to earn something they need or want. Or simply allows someone with something of value to trade it for something they need.

PERENNIALS: FLOWERS ARE GOING TO RISE

As I write this, night has fallen over our home in Alpine. I have the window open, and the scent of lilacs is heavy in the air. It is just past the average last-frost date for our valley—May 18—and our garden is full of texture and color. Tulips have been blooming since Easter, the rhubarb resemble elephant ears, the allium and grape hyacinths have a Dr. Suess quality, the Jacob's ladder is just breaking into royal purple, and the pansies are Expressionist art.

And I haven't lifted a finger.

Thank you, perennials! The workhorse of the garden, perennials are more relevant than ever. They save water in a time when we are all learning to conserve. They need little or no fertilizer in a time when we are learning how phosphorus is damaging local lakes. They thrive on benign neglect when our days are scheduled to the hilt. And they are a bargain, saving time and effort, returning faithfully year after year—and

Tulips seem to bring life back to the garden each spring. The author has planted 100 or more bulbs each fall for many years.

the selection from commercial vendors gets better every summer season. Here are tips for rethinking perennials in your garden:

A SUMMER OF BLOOMS

More than ever, perennials are going head-to-head with annuals to provide a full summer of blooms—gaillardia, in both Indian blanket and burgundy varieties; penstemon in firecracker, cobalt and purple; yarrow in pastel or the new true red varieties. The color choices in ever-blooming daylilies are now hundreds. Cosmos (annuals that faithfully reseed) come in a startling array of colors and petal designs. Johnson's Blue geraniums are prolific. These are my must-haves. Ask the local garden center for recommendations—or better yet, ask your friends and neighbors to share a start with you.

THE NO-COST PIONEER FLOWER NURSERY

Perennials are eminently sharable. Give away starts from your own established plants, and don't be afraid to ask for a start from a neighbor's plant that catches your eye.

To "clone" a perennial, simply use a shovel to remove a portion of the plant. This is best done in early spring or late autumn, when the plants are dormant. Make a clean cut from the parent plant, and dig deeply under the start to leave intact as much of the root system as possible. After planting in the new location, water the plant in well, and then give a good daily watering until new growth shows you the plant has begun to establish itself.

(top left) Perennial echinachea (purple coneflower) and white yarrow frame annual zinnias. (top right) Spikes of purple perennials draw beneficial bees and butterflies. If you look closely, you can see a bee drinking nectar. (bottom) Close-up of a purple coneflower just before coming into full bloom.

Using this simple pioneer method. I have successfully transplanted:

- Grape vines
- Yarrow
- Raspberries
- Rhubarb
- Strawberries
- Daisies
- Purple cone flower
- Black-eyed Susans
- Hostas
- Spiderwort
- All kinds of bulbs
- Cosmos
- Buttercups
- Daylilies
- First-year hollyhocks
- Perennial herbs
- Columbines
- Ornamental grasses
- Creeping phlox
- Mint
- Pansies
- Butterfly weed
- Moss

With a little care, this method even works for transplanting young garden vegetables. If you have a volunteer vegetable that you want to keep but need to move, if you want to share a self-seeding lettuce with a neighbor, or need to consolidate the pole beans closer to the trellis, transplanting is the answer. Even annual flowers can be moved this way. Because the root systems on annual plants are more fragile than established perennials, annuals should never be divided—instead, just move the entire plant. While perennials can be divided without the soaking the soil, annuals do much better in soil that is thoroughly wet, both before moving and after planting in the new location.

Perennial daffodils give an early pop of color to a border in the author's garden. Putting perennials in your garden means years of flowers with very little work.

The first step when transplanting annuals and vegetables is to prepare the hole in the new location first. Make sure the hole is larger and deeper than the root ball of the plant you intend to move. Once the hole is dug, fill with water.

When moving an annual or vegetable plant, the root ball must be kept intact or the plant will die. To do this, carefully insert a garden shovel as deeply as possible into the soil with your foot, taking care not to lift the soil when removing the blade. Lifting the soil at this point can rip the root ball and kill the plant. To be sure I don't move the soil, I put one gloved hand between the plant and the shovel, pressing the ground down firmly as I pull the shovel blade out of the ground. You can also do this with your foot if there is room to safely maneuver without crushing any part of the plant. Repeating this step, cut a circle around the plant. Once the circle is complete, put the shovel back into one of the cuts you've made in the soil, and carefully lift the entire root ball out of the ground.

At the new location, place the annual or vegetable into the wet hole you prepared in advance. Back-fill around the plant with loose soil, and then use the handle of your shovel to gently but firmly tamp down the new soil around the root ball. Do not tamp the root ball itself as this will damage it. Then soak the soil around the plant again. You may want to water the transplant three or four times the first and second days, as the hair roots re-establish themselves in the new location, and then once a day until new growth shows that the plant has taken to its new home. One caution: I would not recommend trying this on taproot vegetables, such as beets, turnips, or rutabaga; even if you were able to keep the taproot intact, any damage to the hair roots on the taproot would likely kill the plant. Using this method, I have successfully transplanted several young specimens:

- Corn (up to 18 inches tall)
- Pole and bush beans (up to 24 inches tall)
- Squash (within the first month)
- Cabbages and broccoli (within the first month)
- Lettuce (up to maturity)
- Pak Choi (within the first month)

THE VICTORIAN AGE

I grew up in a Victorian profusion of flowers, the last remnants of Utah's original pioneer gardens. To my grandmothers, great-aunts, and neighbors, summer meant pastoral Monet blooms. Today, those gardens have often given way to dyed bark mulch surrounding dwarf bushes on drip lines. Thankfully, this tiresome trend is on its way out—Monet is making a comeback. If your yard is still suffering the manicured blues, rip out your weed fabric in favor of Dame's rocket, delphiniums, Nikko blue hydrangea, hyssop, hostas, Easter lilies, butterfly bushes, salvia, and blue-and-golds. See how good it feels—and looks—to color vigorously outside the lines.

The author's perennial garden overflows with color -- and never has to be replanted.

SEED YOUR WAY

Many perennials are surprisingly easy to start indoors. And if you're not ready to put seed trays in a window, local farm stores have great deals—one local store sold 4-inch perennials for a dollar apiece one spring. I took home forty.

THE INCREDIBLE, EDIBLE 'ENNIAL

Strawberries are a superb border plant with magnificent crimped leaves and ermine flowers—and once you have tasted the pure sugar of a sun-warmed strawberry, everything in the grocery store will taste flat. A showy hedge all summer, we have so many raspberries that we can never pick them all. Purple, white, and red grapes by the gross, and over the past several years I've added blackberries. The birds take some, but we have enough to spare—and we like to watch the birds.

THE WATER GARDEN

Perennials rule our backyard pond too. Already elegantly topping the water's surface, our lily pads will be there until the water freezes in late fall. White, red, and pink lilies will surprise us throughout the summer. And just two days ago, our arrowhead plant uncurled its first leathery-green leaf. Zebra reeds spike up from beside a boulder, and on the oppose bank, cattails are profuse. All of these return year after year without a lick of work on my part.

A view of the author's backyard pond. This pond was created years ago using only sheets of inexpensive 6-mil plastic sheeting from a local hardware store. Perennial water lilies bloom every year in pink, red, and white.

(top left) A walkway between two rows of raspberries in the author's backyard, flanked by daisies, Easter lilies, and yarrow. (bottom left) Perennial moss sends delicate fingers down a rock wall. (right) Tulips dazzle with bold colors.

PERENNIAL MISTAKES

Several years ago I bought two evening primroses and planted them in my perennial border near one of the vegetable garden plots. Each year since, those two plants have turned into at least twenty square feet, invading my vegetable bed, perennial bed, and pathway. I have ruthlessly dug them out, but they always return. I may never get rid of them because they are so aggressive. I finally gave up this year and decided to just enjoy the summer-long sea of pink flowers. A hundred years after I'm dead, this tenacious perennial will still probably be happily blooming.

MOSS AS ZEN CARPET

Before you shake your head, saying moss is impossible in the West, think again. True, we have to grow it on a sprinkler system. But the benefits are easy to see—I have two varieties in a short dry creek, and they have thrived and spread to become a tight, attractive ground cover. Nothing else is as meditative and relaxing—and the tiny flowers are exquisite.

Droplets from an early spring rain weigh down the heads of tulips in the author's spring garden. If you plant an abundance of tulips and daffodils, you won't feel even a twinge of guilt cutting some to take to the kitchen table!

PERENNIAL FAITH

As a youth I dug tulips from the abandoned post office one town over and planted them along our collapsed garage. Some emerged that spring; I imagine they still do. In Alpine, I have planted a hundred bulbs each fall for nearly a decade now. Last year I planted after dark, beating the first snow by hours. The promise of bulbs and all perennials is that whatever may happen, taking another year in hand, flowers are going to rise.

(right top) Easter lilies in full bloom surround a ceramic bird bath in the author's perennial flower garden. This kind of perennial design brings touches of tranquility to the garden without the need to plant new flowers each year. (right bottom) Available in a huge array of autumn colors, hardy chrysanthemums end the flower season in October in the way that tulips herald the season in April. Don't be fooled by cheap mums on sale in big-box stores in September. If you want them to really be hardy, they need to be planted in spring to have the whole season to develop roots.

CHAPTER 16

TAKING A SECOND LOOK AT FRESH EGGS

For homesteaders, the role that eggs played in self-sufficiency cannot be overstated. They still provide this service for some families today.

The once-common backyard flocks may be gone forever, for several reasons. Self-sufficient living is no longer a focus for most families. Fewer families have space for chickens because of shrinking home-lot size and the popularity of condominiums and townhomes. Where there is space, neighbors may not be comfortable with chickens. Fewer people have knowledge about how or why to keep chickens. And even fewer people want to dedicate time to producing homegrown food.

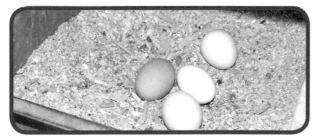

Eggs waiting to be gathered. The author's chicken coop features a bank of zinc nesting boxes inherited from the author's grandfather, Phill Nielson, who once owned a commercial eggery in Lynndyl, Utah, with three thousand hens.

This last reason should be your first consideration if you are a family interested in keeping chickens. Chicken keeping is a commitment, like adding any animal to the family. When deciding if a few hens are right for you, there are pros and cons that every family should know.

Cons:

- Healthy chickens live in clean coops. This means someone must muck out the manure and haul it to the family garden or compost bin.
- Chickens need access to water and food, despite sweltering heat, freezing cold, family vacations, or family emergencies.
- Chickens rely on their human owners to keep them safe.
- Chicks require special care and feeding.

Pros:

- Chickens provide eggs. For families, *ahem*, truly inspired with the homesteading spirit (take a deep breath, dear reader), they could even help stock the family freezer.
- Chickens provide excellent free garden fertilizer.
- Excess eggs can be sold for a small income.

- Caring for chickens can connect adults and children to where food comes from, the link between labor and food, the cycle of life, and the benefits of self-sufficient living. In my experience, children exposed to this knowledge become the most likely adults to not only practice this received wisdom but to pass it on as well.

HOW THE BACKYARD CHICKEN FLOCK DISAPPEARED

Despite growing up surrounded by chickens, I had never seen a broody hen or a natural-born chick until my wife and I got our chickens.

"We human keepers of poultry have made it emphatically clear to modern hens that their mothering instincts are not welcome," wrote Harvey Ussery in *Backyard Poultry* magazine. "That is, we consider broodiness a big nuisance, since a hen who is broody is not laying . . . so have selected against this natural instinct in modern breeds. If we are going to make going broody a capital offense, it doesn't take long for the hens to get the point!"

As a youth in Lynndyl, Utah (population 98), we never had chickens on our farm, for good reason—we didn't need them. My mother's parents, who lived just up the road from the farm, had two flocks of snow-white Leghorns. In the 1960s, they operated a commercial eggery with two to three thousand hens, wholesaling thousands of eggs each week. With six daughters to feed, my grandfather started the egg business to supplement his work in real estate.

As young teens, my mother and her sisters were allowed to drive the family car half a block to the egg houses. They knocked on the egg house door to warn the chickens they were coming in; otherwise, "they would fly at us and attack us," my mother recalled to me. She and her sisters filled ten wire baskets twice a day, sometimes pecked by hens, which did not want their eggs taken.

In the beginning, Grandma Nielson and her girls washed all the eggs in the kitchen sink, using sandpaper blocks to remove any dirt before packing them in cardboard flats of thirty. They looked for rare double-yokers or soft eggs with shells like paper, the first egg laid by a newly mature hen. Twice a week Grandpa drove the eggs twenty miles to a cooperative where they were added to other local eggs. Advertised as "milk-white," the eggs were shipped from California to New York.

When in their mid-eighties, I asked my grandparents to recall their long-ago egg "empire."

"You got in the baskets and you were having the time of your life," my grandmother, Billie Nielson, started in immediately. "Do you remember that?" As a three-year-old, I had snuck onto the back porch one afternoon where the eggs were waiting for cleaning. When I was found, I was "pitching eggs at everything,

A mother hen tends to her newborn chicks in the author's backyard. Having hens who hatch out chicks is one of the best parts of living the self-sufficient life.

trees and everything," my grandma recalled. "You got in trouble."

I didn't invent the sport. My mother later told me with a laugh that occasionally, when her two youngest daughters were bored, Grandma would let them throw eggs at the house, washing the red brick down with the hose afterward.

After a few months of washing eggs by hand, Grandpa bought an automatic egg washer. A basket of eggs was placed in its center as water and a "special solution" purchased from the co-op spun around the eggs.

"I thought I had the world by the tail," my grandmother recalled.

Once a year, the girls went into the chicken coop with special hooked sticks to catch the two-year-old hens by the leg, delivering them to Grandpa upside-down. Because the hens' egg production were beginning to decline, Grandpa chopped their heads off, and the girls plucked, gutted and quartered the hens, often finding yet-to-be-laid eggs in the carcass. The birds went into the family freezer.

My mother recalled that with eggs abounding, my grandmother "would try to think of anything she could make with eggs. She would bake angel-food cake by the houseful." To this day, my mother has a hard time eating eggs.

My grandparents had given up their huge commercial eggery by the time I was born but kept a hundred hens for home use. These hens lived in a huge barracks purchased from the Topaz Japanese Interment Camp, where Japanese-Americans from California were detained during World War II in Utah's West Desert. The hens never went outside. From these my grandmother sold eggs for 60 cents a dozen to neighbors who came, carton in hand, to the back door chatting about who in town was dying, marrying, going to jail, or prospering conspicuously. Because of Grandma's eggs, we rarely ever bought any from the store.

A "Buff Orpington" hen wanders the author's pasture. Free-range hens have been shown to produce healthier eggs.

The idea of me having a broody hen was foreign to my Lynndyl grandparents, who had always purchased their chicks from the feed store.

"Oh well, there is nothing you can do about that," said my grandma upon hearing the news, assuming I was upset that egg production would be disrupted. She wondered where I had gotten fertilized eggs.

"Oh, you have a rooster," she said when I explained. "You *are* well off. You're in the chicken business now."

In Sigurd, Utah, my Warnock grandparents also had hens for household eggs, as did my great-grandma Lexia, who lived a minute's walk from their house down the red clay country road. Visiting Sigurd (population 200) as a child, I'd rush to my great-grandmother Lexia's house, afraid she'd gather the eggs before she knew I was there. She kept her hens in a converted granary, and they had a large outdoor run. I remember cradling eggs to her kitchen, feeling like my hands were full of gold coins.

Great-grandma Lexia had been a commercial egg

producer, keeping 250 layers for 20 years, long before I was born. Gathering about 200 eggs a day, she sold them to the Utah Poultry Cooperative.

As it turned out, asking my Grandpa Warnock about my great-grandmother's eggs turned out to be our last conversation. Days later, he died. Fourteen hours before his funeral, my grandma, his wife of sixty-three years, died of heartbreak. The morticians and florists worked all night to allow a double funeral; we buried them side by side in the red clay.

Having our first broody hen, "I've learned a lot," I wrote in my journal. "Old eggs float, eggs shouldn't be washed to avoid cleaning off their natural protective covering, called the bloom, and the shells can be crushed and fed back as calcium to the hens."

Commercial egg farms, I learned, wash their eggs and then spray them with mineral oil to replace the bloom and give the eggs a shine.

After the rush to industrialize egg hatcheries following World War II, many traditional breeds of chickens were abandoned for modern hybrids and then became extinct. Other breeds were brought to the brink of vanishing. Recognizing this loss of heritage and generations of work, seven hundred members of the Society for the Preservation of Poultry Antiquities now raise endangered chickens in the United States, working for the past four decades to ensure no more breeds disappear.

"In 1868 Charles Darwin published an inventory of chicken breeds existing at the time—all thirteen of them," writes Gail Damerow. "Most of the breeds we know today were developed since then. Unfortunately, this incredible genetic diversity has fallen victim to the whims of fowl fads."[1]

Chicken breeds and varieties flourished in the United States between 1875 and 1925, Damerow says, but beginning in the 1930s, two things quashed that: new zoning laws began to prohibit backyard flocks,

and commercial egg and poultry meat farms began to flourish.

For 250 years, ending with World War II, "80 to 90 percent of American households kept chickens to supplement their diet and their annual cash income, as it was easy to sell extra eggs locally," writes Jay Rossier. "Before mass-production methods came to agriculture, the goal was a hen that laid well for as long as possible and that produced offspring that would flesh out well for the stew pot or roasting oven."[2]

Commercial farms developed hybrid "fast-growing birds with broad breasts, big legs and thighs, and rich yellow skin," writes Will Graves. "In 1934, about 30 million broilers were produced in the United States. In 1983, over two billion broilers were raised. In the 1930s, it took about five pounds of feed to put one pound of gain on a broiler chicken over a period of four months. . . . Now, in the 1980s, it only takes two pounds of feed to produce one pound of weight gain on a broiler chicken."

"We have reached the absurd situation where there are children today who eat chicken nuggets but have never seen a live chicken," writes Carlo Petrini. "We have completely severed the link which until after World War II tied people to the earth with respect to food."

Today, many cities, petitioned by residents, are allowing hens in residential areas once again. Some of this interest is certainly a fad that will pass—think of backyard bomb shelters.

Another segment of the public interest is certainly a response to the sputtering economy, rising food and fuel prices, and a renewed craving for the security that comes with true self-sufficient living. For the first time in nearly a century, families have lost homes and jobs in frightening numbers, and even families whose finances have escaped unscathed are jittery because they've seen friends, neighbors, and extended family members struggle. More families are being called on—and relied on—to help extended family members. People are beginning to remember that gardens and chickens, not grocery stores, were once the mainstays of the family budget. Our collective memory of previous national struggles is renewed, and we remember that in the Great Depression, often those least affected had resources to provide for themselves. And during World War II, when the United States was rationing food for the first and only time in the industrial age, so-called family Victory Gardens pulled the nation through.

Increasingly, families are also concerned about health. The number of commercial food recalls seems to be rising—remember the recent recalls of spinach, tomatoes, and beef?—and has deservedly drawn a lot of media attention. An increasing number of people want to know how their food was raised, even how the chickens that produced their eggs were fed and housed. Or how fruits and vegetables were fertilized, whether they were chemically treated for weeds and pests or chemically encouraged to ripen. More families are looking for local producers, where they can see how and where their food was raised. More people are beginning to feel that food security, both personally and as a nation, must be connected once again in some degree to American small-scale producers.

The world has changed since the lives of our forbearers. But self-provident living continues to offer security and peace of mind to those who practice it.

Note

1. Damerow, *Storey's Guide to Raising Chickens.*
2. Rossier, *Living with Chickens.*
3. Graves, *Raising Poultry Successfully.*
4. Petrini, *Slow Food Nation: Why Our Food Should Be Good, Clean, and Fair.*

A "White Leghorn" hen wanders among fall grasses. White leghorns produce more eggs—about 300 per year per hen—than any other variety, and they are great winter layers even without any artificial light or heat.

CHAPTER 17

WHAT EVERY FAMILY SHOULD KNOW WHEN CONSIDERING HEN-KEEPING

At our house, we've made a lot of mistakes over the years of chicken keeping. I share those so that, should you decide to give fresh eggs a try, your experience will be less bumpy.

Around Christmas in the third year of our marriage, my wife mentioned we ought to get hens to give us eggs.

Purchasing baby chicks to raise is more work than letting the mother hen do the job, if you can. Here, chicks warm themselves under a heat lamp in an outdoor enclosure in April.

When spring came, we bought eight-day-old chicks for $2.50 apiece at our local feed store and immediately made our first mistake: choosing to keep them in an open cardboard box with a heat light in our master bathroom for several weeks. Not knowing any better, we thought this was how it had to be done. It doesn't. Chicks do just fine outside as early as April, as long as they have a very low hanging light bulb (traditional, not energy-saving) to huddle around at night. We've now raised many chicks by keeping them outside from the moment we get them, and we've never lost one, even on bitter nights.

About a week after we got those first chicks, I mentioned them to coworkers in idle conversation. One woman immediately soured. Her face twisted as if I had announced I was cultivating the Black Plague in a home laboratory. "What do you want chickens for?"

"For eggs," I blurted, momentarily unsure of myself.

"You won't save any money," she said. "It's cheaper to get eggs from the store."

"I know." This wasn't much of a defense, but it was all I could think to say.

Today, I can answer this question far more

Various breeds of chickens surround a half-White Leghorn, half-who-knows-what rooster in the author's barnyard. Roosters keep a careful eye on free-range hens, who otherwise are prone to wander far and wide.

clearly, starting first of all by refuting the notion that homegrown eggs are more expensive than store-bought. This can be true. For a time, this was true for us, a result of not knowing what we were doing. Today our eggs are free; even better, they bring in income.

FEEDING YOUR FLOCK

Feeding chickens has become a major concern recently after Utah garnered national attention when a Utah County family suffered arsenic poisoning from home-raised eggs.

According to media reports, tests showed that the family's two children had very high arsenic levels, far beyond what government statistics deem safe. An extensive investigation by the Utah County Health Department concluded the arsenic was coming from the commercial chicken feed the family was giving to their laying hens. Unbelievably, media reports found that not only is arsenic a common additive to the food (called mash) fed to both commercial and backyard layers across the United States, it is legal

under federal law. The conglomerates that sell the mash have reportedly lobbied Congress for decades to keep the law intact, citing data showing arsenic to be safe because it does not affect the chickens and is not passed on through the eggs to humans. The Utah County Health Department determination was reportedly the first of its kind in the nation to state that in fact arsenic as an additive in chicken feed was the scientifically documented cause of two human arsenic poisoning cases. As of the writing of this book, the aftermath of this investigation and report remain to be seen.

This news was a wake-up call for families that get their eggs from the grocery store and for families who have believed they were raising healthy eggs at home.

Over the past several years, discussion in the poultry-keeping community has increasingly focused on the fact that families who must rely on outside sources to feed their chickens are really not much more self-reliant than families relying on the grocery store for eggs.

Beyond arsenic, there has been growing concern about another additive in chicken feed—antibiotics. For decades, antibiotics have been a common ingredient in commercial chicken food, used to counter the massive disease outbreaks associated with keeping so many chickens—tens and hundreds of thousands—industrially warehoused in close quarters without access to pasture or fresh air.

In a Feb. 10, 2002, article titled "Poultry Industry Quietly Cuts Back On Antibiotic Use," the *New York Times* reported that 26.6 million pounds of antibiotics were fed to feedlot animals in the United States each year, and that the *New England Journal of Medicine* had published studies the previous October confirming a link between the overuse of antibiotics in feedlot animals and drug resistant bacteria found in meat and poultry.

In a 2002 article titled "Playing Chicken With Our Antibiotics," *Time* magazine reported that the number of certain human infections immune to antibiotics had jumped from negligible to 18 percent within three years because of overuse of antibiotics in poultry feedlots. That spike so alarmed the federal government that the Food and Drug Administration asked large pharmaceutical companies to stop selling the drugs to poultry farmers, but at least one major drug producer protested that request. According to other media reports, some of the largest companies selling poultry have begun to reduce their use of antibiotics after national media attention surrounding the issue.[1]

To me, all of this illustrates how truly difficult it has become for the public to trace the origins of our mass-produced food. Chicken feed purchased at farm stores often comes without any labeling of what ingredients may have been added. My local farm store was not immediately sure where the feed was manufactured and packaged and said no nutritional or ingredient information was available.

For families who need to buy commercial feed for their chickens but don't want additives, purchasing cracked corn from the farm store should be a safe bet, though it doesn't hurt to ask if the corn has been treated with antibiotics or anything else. You could also purchase whole wheat in bulk from the grocery store.

The difference between laying mash and cracked corn purchased from farm stores is that mash has been ground to a powder to make it faster for the chickens, particularly in commercial feedlots, to digest. Additives have often been mixed into the powder.

For years I purchased commercial chicken feed, but now I have found ways to directly control what my chickens eat by feeding them wheat. Better yet, free wheat. By offering to take old food storage wheat and beans from anyone looking to update their supplies, I have been given large quantities of grain to supply my flock with food.

A black-and-white Barred Plymouth Rock hen searches for bugs in the grass under an apple tree, flanked by two Buff Orpingtons. The author believes that if most people saw the conditions of the chickens which lay grocery-store eggs, they would never eat eggs again.

Chickens readily eat whole-kernel wheat, corn, buckwheat, and other grains that have not been ground up. Backyard gardeners with enough space can grow at least some food for their chickens and can purchase the rest as whole grains rather than processed mash feed. Chickens can also be fed sprouted or boiled beans, any vegetable scraps from the kitchen, and stale bread.

Just this evening, I took five medium carrots, four small beets, and a small zucchini from the garden, sliced them all thinly, sautéed them for about four minutes with a daub of butter and drizzle of olive oil, and served this as a side dish for supper. The carrot tops, beet tops, peelings, and zucchini ends went into the chicken bowl. After supper, there were some leftovers, and this too went into the chicken bowl, along with some stale potato chips someone discovered forgotten in a cupboard, and some bread crusts left by our four-year-old grandson after lunch. Saving every possible scrap to feed the chickens quickly reveals just how much a family otherwise sends to the landfill. Even my elderly neighbors, not wanting to waste old food, regularly bring me stale bread, rolls, and even cake to feed my chickens. Watching chickens attack a cake with gusto is a rare sight to see. After the ward Christmas dinner last year, our bishop asked me to take home to my chickens all the leftover dinner rolls that he had not been able to give away to ward members. People appreciate knowing that food is not going to waste.

For those who have the space, allowing chickens to range in a pasture, fallow garden, or weed patch allows the chickens to work for their own food, which is their natural instinct. Chickens keep down the population of grasshoppers and other bugs, and they are never happier than when they are scratching through weeds and dirt. Chickens will even greedily eat that baseball bat-sized zucchini you don't know what to do with.

Pioneer Stories

Chickens in Sevier County, Utah, circa 1898

In her memoirs, my great-grandmother, Lexia Dastrup Warnock, 1890–1985, recalled trying to guard the family hens in her childhood in Sigurd, Utah. "Mother had a flock of chickens and we children used to watch for hawks and coyotes, to scare them away, but we lost lots of chickens anyway. The grass of the pasture was littered with feathers left from the coyotes' meals."

Another entry in her memoir details her brothers having mischief with the family chicken flock: "I remember finding Leland and Homer and Horace laughing at the antics of our old mother hens with a dozen baby chicks. The poor hen was trying to perform her motherly duties but couldn't walk naturally because they had fed her bread soaked in some brandy they found. Poor hens! The boys had fun!"

Knowing how much to feed your chickens is a matter of experiment and experience. I feed my dozen chickens about a cup of wheat a day during spring, summer, and fall—not one cup per bird, but one cup total. With more than an acre of pasture, they should mostly feed themselves during these months.

In winter, when range food is far less available, I increase their grain ration, depending on the temperature and what kitchen scraps I have to offer them that day. Chickens should never be fed just kitchen scraps in winter. Be sure they get enough vegetable protein in winter to adequately keep up their body temperature. Feed them generously when the weather is below freezing. On bitter nights, feed them an hour or two before nightfall.

A hen peers out from the tiny doorway of the coop, on her way out to range in the grasses of the pasture.

THE BASIC HOUSING OF CHICKENS

The first flock of chickens my wife and I owned after we were married came to an ignoble end. One winter night, we forgot to close the coop door and woke to find that some winter-hungry predator had taken four hens—half our flock. Weeks later a miscommunication left the door open another night, and three of the remaining four were killed, leaving only feathers as evidence of the struggle. Taking pity on our single remaining chicken, a neighbor gave us a companion for it, but both were killed soon after by hawks while they wandered around the yard.

The next spring, when we purchased chicks to replace our flock, a raccoon dug an enormous hole under the coop wall the first night, taking four chicks. That same day, I bought four more and sandbagged the coop, foolishly thinking this would end the problem. The next morning a new hole had appeared,

and two chicks were taken. We kept the remaining seven in my home office until, at three weeks old, they had grown enough to jump out of the box.

Moving them outside, we stationed our dog beside the coop each night, which worked perfectly. We finally solved the problem by tacking chicken wire around the outside of the coop, creating a sort of skirt about two feet out on all sides so predators could not burrow under.

THE COOP

Security from predators and shelter from the elements are the main needs of poultry. This can be as simple as a structure built from scrap plywood and old boards, or something quite fancy. For keeping chicks, we use a small "chick" coop next door to the main coop which has doubled as a rabbit hutch. For our main coop, we used plywood and lumber to convert one end of our barn. I have a friend in Provo who built a makeshift coop and small run, completely enclosed in chicken wire, for her backyard flock of six or so hens. Be as creative and decorative or rustic as you like.

CLEANING THE COOP

How often you clean your coop depends on your operation. I know of chicken keepers whose flock never leave their small coop and so the coop is cleaned once a week. Others use a mobile coop that can be dragged or rolled around, enabling them to move the entire coop and flock to a new spot of clean earth each week. Because my chickens free-range outdoors most of the day, except during days with deep snow, I clean my coop only two or three times a year, always in the spring and fall. Using a square-nosed shovel, I scrape the roosts. The chickens are outside ranging the pasture while I do this. Using a garden shovel, I then remove four to six inches from the floor. This is loose soil made up of a combination of feathers, pine shavings, dirt, and dried manure. I remove everything that is loose, down to the hardpan dirt below. All of this is either shoveled onto a tarp and dragged to the garden in small loads, or pitched into a wheelbarrow and carted to the garden. Here I spread it out and till it under.

After cleaning out the chicken manure, I take a small hand-pump sprayer, available at any farm or hardware store, and spray down the entire coop with a well-diluted bleach water—stalls, nest boxes, roosts, everything. Then I lock the coop for a couple of hours while this dries, just to make sure the chickens are

A mother hen keeps a serious eye on one of "her" chicks. In truth, when one hen becomes broody, the other hens in the coop all lay eggs in her nest, and she hatches out the children of many hens. Talk about volunteering your time!

not exposed to the bleach water. This is also a good time to take out the waterer and clean it with a bleach solution too.

A friend with chickens once asked me how I got rid of the feathers from the manure before spreading it in the garden. Feathers are a rich source of nitrogen and I was happy to put my friend's mind at ease—feathers should definitely be tilled into the garden.

THE ROOST (SLEEPING QUARTERS)

The coop will need a roost, which is a high shelf or board for the chickens to sleep on. They feel safest, and do best, when they have this kind of perch for sleeping. I have several in my coop, starting at four feet high, then six feet, with the highest at eight feet. Nothing fancier than a level board is required.

Ivy hangs from the walls of the chicken coop, keeping them green year-round. This ivy has crept over from the other side of the barn wall, which is covered in ivy. The chickens need nest boxes to lay eggs in, and high perches for nighttime roosting.

NEST BOXES (FOR EGG LAYING)

You will need several nest boxes, approximately one box per every three or four hens. They simply provide some kind of semi-private place where a hen can lay her egg, are usually open to the air on only one side, and can be purchased or built. I've used old apple boxes but now have the original zinc nest boxes that my grandparents used in their Lynndyl coop. Modern versions of plastic or tin can cost a couple hundred dollars today, but the investment might be well worth the money: mine have now been in service for decades in our family.

Different people prefer to line their nest boxes with different things. Having used straw for several years, I now prefer pine shavings, which are inexpensive at any farm store. Both compost nicely, but shavings keep the eggs cleaner, are easier to put in and take out, smell better, and are far less dusty than straw. My chickens enjoyed kicking the straw out of the nest boxes, forcing me to refill often, but this was solved with pine shavings.

If your coop is a walk-in room like ours, gathering the eggs means opening the door and going inside, which is a good daily opportunity to check on the living conditions generally. Many people use much smaller coops; in that case, nest boxes are usually built to be accessed from the outside.

AIR FLOW

Air circulation vents dust and odor. I have a north-facing window covered with rabbit wire. Glass windows should be avoided, as the chickens are likely to break them, even if they are covered with chicken wire. It may seem counter-intuitive, but there is no need for windows that shut, even in winter. Be sure, however, that your hens are not directly exposed to wind and weather; they must have a place within the coop to escape the elements while roosting.

WATER

I recommend buying the largest waterer you can find, as this will dramatically reduce the number of times you must refill it in the blazing heat of summer and bitter freeze of winter. It will cost more in the beginning, but you will thank yourself over the years. It is possible to make your own gravity-fed waterer; instructions appear now and then in poultry-related magazines and on the Internet. Here's one reason to consider buying one instead of making one: an electric waterer in winter keep the water slightly above freezing.

For many years, we never used an electric waterer. I variously gave the chickens fresh water every day, or shoveled snow into the coop for them to eat. There is ongoing debate over using snow to "water" chickens in winter, and these debates have played out in *Backyard Poultry* magazine in particular. Some chicken owners feel using only snow is possibly unhealthy and perhaps even cruel. Others point out that chickens and other animals have historically eaten snow as a source of winter water. I have fed my chickens fresh snow each day for weeks, with no other source of water, and the chickens have thrived. They gobble up the snow and swallow it. Even when they have full access to water, they choose on their own to eat snow while free-ranging during winter—I've witnessed this many times.

Where we live in central Utah, it is not uncommon to go weeks without seeing the temperature rise above freezing in the depths of winter. Keeping water constantly available to chickens without electricity is impossible, just as it was for those who settled this state. When the snow is two feet deep, the chickens won't go out in it anyway, so there is sometimes a stretch of weeks where my otherwise free-range chickens are cooped up. Foregoing fresh water in favor of throwing them several large shovelfuls of fresh, clean snow once or twice a day during these times has not affected their health, decreased their egg laying, or stressed them in any way that I have discerned.

Sometimes stretches of below-freezing weather occur where there is little or no fresh, clean snow to give the chickens. In these cases, I have taken a couple of gallons of water from the house to the chickens each day in a bucket. I pour the water into a six-inch-deep rubber tub, available at any farm store. The water freezes over in about an hour, and the chickens drink it until then. In the evening, I break the ice so they can drink a second time, or on truly bitter days when the water has frozen solid, I turn the rubber tub upside down outside the coop, replace the tub, and refill it.

To make this kind of system successful, you must be home. Last winter we needed to leave for several days during the worst part of winter, and so I broke down and purchased my first electric-heated chicken waterer, which cost forty dollars. It holds three gallons, which lasts my dozen chickens a week. And it worked well. The thing was not fun to refill— this requires turning it upside down and filling it with a hose through a small hole in the bottom, which is then plugged with a rubber stopper before the whole contraption is turned right-side-up again to allow gravity feeding of water.

In summer, a large gravity-fed waterer works very well. All gravity-fed containers must be leveled, either by suspending them from the roof by a chain so they hang a few inches above the floor, or by placing them on raised bricks. I use both methods. The suspension method has the advantage of being spill-proof; using bricks, it is possible, and probable, that the chickens will knock the whole thing over once in a while.

However you give it to them, the water should be as clean as possible. The waterer can be scrubbed as needed with a brush; I often use a handful of grass. Occasional cleaning with bleach water is recommended, but be sure to rinse it thoroughly afterward. Never feed bleach water to chickens—or any other animal, of course.

DUST BATHS

Chickens clean themselves using the same method as horses, cattle, goats, and even dogs and cats when dogs and cats are allowed to be outdoors— the dust bath. In the coop and outdoors, chickens need a shady patch of earth where they can scratch down to create a dust bowl. They will then luxuriate in this dust, rolling and wiggling and spreading their wings, quite a sight to behold. They do this to smother microscopic mites that may infest their feathers otherwise, so dust bathing is important to their overall health.

SELLING EGGS

When we were buying feed-store grain to supply our chickens, my goal was to sell enough eggs each month—eight dozen at two dollars per dozen—to pay for the feed. This provided enough eggs for our family while paying the feed bill. Today I don't pay for feed, as mentioned above, so any money I take in is slowly repaying the cost of chicks, waterers, chicken wire for fencing the pasture, and the screws and the wood used to section off the coop.

Another consideration when selling eggs is whether to buy blank egg cartons—or if you are feeling really fancy, you can even get customized boxes with your family name or "farm" name on them. For years we sold eggs by recycling grocery store egg cartons, simply by asking anyone who wanted eggs to bring their own recycled cartoon.

People quickly started not only bringing their own but giving us extras.

One summer we got really ambitious with our garden and decided to sell fresh produce and eggs at the local farmers market. We knew we needed to sell eggs to help offset the 150 dollar season fee we paid to be part of the market. Problem was, we couldn't sell eggs at a public market using cartons from the grocery store. So I purchased a box of two hundred blank egg cartons from an online vendor for forty dollars, which included shipping. At the market, we sold those eggs for three dollars a dozen, and they sold out within the first hour every single weekend, mostly because we never had more than four dozen to sell at a time.

It's now been two years since we bought those two hundred egg cartons, and we have not used even fifty of them yet. This is because while we continue to sell eggs, we ask our customers to bring back their cartons, and they do this faithfully, reusing the same carton over and over as long as it is still clean and functional.

Here is some advice learned the hard way— when selling eggs, start out in the way you intend to continue. Changing the price, once established, is not easy. We never intended to sell eggs. I thought it would be a bother, and so we always planned to just have enough for our household. But it quickly became obvious that we would have more eggs than we could use, and when we got to the point where we had eight dozen eggs in the fridge, I changed my mind about selling eggs. First, we gave them away to select friends and neighbors, too embarrassed to ask for any money. Of course finding a home for free, fresh, free-range eggs took no effort at all. Since I was paying for the feed, I quickly realized that supplying free eggs to the neighborhood was not a display of financial acumen. We hesitantly began asking for $1 a dozen, explaining that we wanted to offset the cost of feed. No one blinked. That is when I realized that selling a few dozen eggs each month could easily pay the entire cost of feeding the chickens, if I could muster the courage to charge two dollars a dozen. Rather than being greedy, I felt this was provident living—after all, I gathered the eggs, washed the eggs, purchased the cartons, packaged the eggs, fed and watered the hens, let them out each morning, locked them up each night, fenced the pasture with chicken wire, built the coop, cleaned the coop, and lined the nest boxes. For all that, selling enough eggs so that our family was essentially getting free eggs was a good trade, I felt.

My only regret is that I didn't start out in the way I intended to go. Telling friends and family that the price was going from zero, to one dollar, and finally two dollars was awkward in several cases.

As for finding customers, I know of no backyard chicken-keeper who has ever had trouble finding people to buy their eggs—and many of them charge up to double what we charge. If sales are slow, give away a dozen to anyone who seems interested, and tell them to go home, crack open one of the eggs next to a store-bought egg, and see the difference. The shells on your eggs will be much thicker. The yolk will be much brighter. The whites will be less watery. When cooked side by side in a frying pan, there is a definite difference in taste. And if your eggs are produced from free-range chickens, as ours are, you can share this information with them, from the February/March 2009 issue of *Mother Earth News* magazine:

> The results are coming in from Mother Earth News' latest round of pastured egg nutrient tests. Once again, pastured egg producers are kicking the commercial industry's butt—yippee, go free range! Our previous tests found that eggs from hens raised on pasture—as compared to

Chicken breeds that lay well in winter for us

- White Leghorn
- Barred Plymouth Rock
- Rhode Island Red
- Buff Orpington

Chickens breeds that do not reliably produce winter eggs

- Ameraucanas

the official USDA data for factory-farm eggs—contain:

⅓ less cholesterol
¼ less saturated fat
⅔ more vitamin A
Two times more omega-3 fatty acids
Three times more vitamin E
Seven times more beta carotene

Two "Buff Orpington" hens skirt the author's backyard pond after an early winter snowstorm. To stay warm on bitter winter nights, chickens fluff out their feathers, creating a bulky warm coat for themselves.

Now we are looking at vitamin D, of which many people don't get enough. New research is showing that this common vitamin deficiency may be related to much more than just weak bones—from diabetes and cancer to heart disease and multiple sclerosis(...) Our bodies can get vitamin D in two ways: when sunlight strikes our skin, or from our diet. Eggs are one of a small list of foods that are naturally rich in vitamin D. The USDA says supermarket eggs contain an average of 34 International Units per 100 grams. Our tests of eggs from four pastured farms in Texas, Kansas, Kentucky, and Pennsylvania found that their eggs contained *three to six times as much vitamin D as typical supermarket eggs.* This means two scrambled eggs from pastured hens may give you 63 to 126 percent of the recommended daily intake of 200 IU of vitamin D. You can keep track of our ongoing pastured egg research at www.MotherEarthNews.com/eggs."[2]

THE BACKYARD FLOCK IN WINTER

How the popular wisdom came to believe that chickens won't lay eggs in cold weather, I'll never know. I've had to take people out to the coop with me to prove to them that chickens do indeed lay eggs in winter.

"Oh, you mean they will lay winter eggs if you have a heated coop," several people have said.

I have never heated my coop. I never even used a heated waterer until last winter.

"Then you mean you can force them to lay by leaving a light on all night."

There has never been any light in my coop except natural sunlight.

On several occasions I've had people look at me askance during this kind of conversation, as though they were trying to figure out what kind of trick I was playing on them. I've even been asked if the eggs I sell in winter are hoarded up during the summer. Yikes!

The truth of the matter is this: Egg laying is controlled not at all by temperature, but by day-length, available protein, and breed. Some breeds don't lay eggs in winter. All breeds at least slow down their laying in winter. And all breeds will stop laying in winter (or summer for that matter) if they are not getting enough protein in their diet. Lack of protein also causes feather loss, and even death if chickens are not fed adequately enough to keep up their body temperature on bitter winter nights.

Chickens are naturally equipped to keep themselves warm in winter, if they are correctly fed. They simply huddle together to share body warmth, and puff out their feathers. This puffing traps a layer of warm air between their skin and their feathers, creating an insulating blanket. I have an Ameraucana hen who looks exactly like an owl at night when her feathers are puffed out. The first time I noticed this I actually thought an owl had somehow decided to spend the night cuddled up to my chickens—the sight stopped me dead in my tracks when I was late gathering the eggs. For this alone I think this breed is worth having, although their blue, green, and red eggs are great too.

Some chicken breeds with large or droopy combs (the pointy flap of flesh on the head) and wattles (the flap of flesh below the beak) can suffer frostbite if exposed to prolonged sub-freezing temperatures. This will not harm the chicken's overall health, though it can't feel good. The frost-bitten section may shrivel and fall off naturally. If this is a concern in your area, stick with raising breeds with shorter combs and wattles. To find out which breeds these are, ask your vendor or consult their catalog when ordering.

FREE-RANGE CHICKENS

These chickens are allowed to forage an open area for food for part of the day. This could mean they have an expanse of pasture or fallow garden or weed patch to roam in unrestricted, or it could mean living in a mobile enclosure that is moved to new ground at least once a week.

Free-range chickens should be kept in their coop until at least ten o'clock each morning in order to give them time to lay their eggs. Most eggs are laid in the morning, though some will be laid in the afternoon. Letting them out earlier than this will begin to encourage them to lay their eggs outside, which will make it hard for you to find the eggs and encourage predators.

The great thing about chickens is that once they have been let out to roam, they will put themselves

Two hens take advantage of the last sunlight of the day to roam the pasture, hunting and pecking for food. For three seasons of the year, free-range hens will practically feed themselves if they have access to enough space.

to bed at sundown. Chickens prefer to roost in the same place each night, and if you will provide them with a great roost, they will happily use it. Chickens should be "taught" to identify their new home. If your chickens were raised by their natural mother, she will train them for you. If your chicks were purchased, or if you are given mature chickens by someone looking to get rid of them, you should keep them locked in the coop for four to seven days before letting them free-range the pasture. This time will allow them to "learn" where their home is—where they can roost, get food and water, and lay their eggs. Once they have established routine, they will return to the coop at will throughout the day while free-ranging and will put themselves to bed each night. Of course you will need to let them out each morning, and close their door against predators each night.

If you suddenly find that your chickens are not returning to the coop at night, this is a sure sign that some predator has tried to attack them in their sleep.

A baby chick peeks out from the warmth of her mother's feathers. Mother hens keep their chicks warm during a day of roaming by gathering them under their feathers for a few minutes. And of course they spend the night cozied up in their mother's warm feather blanket.

Check the coop for an unusual amount of feathers, and count your chickens to make sure none have been killed. This kind of night attack happens most often in the early evening hours of winter, when the door to the coop has not been closed soon enough after dark. Normally, predators wait until late at night, when all is quiet and still, to try and take chickens—and if the coop door is securely closed, and you've laid a skirt of chicken wire along the ground outside the walls, you should have no problems. But as winter drags on, hungry predators are emboldened and will sometimes try to enter the coop immediately after dark. It can be easy in the early nightfall of winter to neglect closing the door at dusk, but if you find your animals refusing to return to the coop, this is likely the cause. If you've been careful about closing the door and you still have this problem, scour the coop for cracks, tunnels, or other openings where ermine or mink could be getting in at night.

MOTHER HENS (CALLED BROODY HENS)

Three years after we got our first chicks, on Thursday, July 12, 2007, I forgot to gather the eggs. When I got back to the coop late the next night, I found a black hen still sitting in one of the nest boxes. I shooed her twice, but she didn't move. It wasn't until she pecked at me as I tried to lift her out that I realized what was happening.

That night, I read for hours on the Internet, researching chicken motherhood, poring over articles with titles like "Working with Broody Hens: Let Mama Do It" and "Robyn's Chicken Breeding Page."

You can always tell when a hen turns broody because she will stay in a nest box overnight instead of roosting. Over the years, I've learned that a broody hen must be moved into a private space the very first night of the brood. Otherwise, the tumult of the chicken coop is likely to distract her and she will "break her brood" sooner or later. Usually soon. Of course, if you have a broody hen but you don't want to hatch out chicks for any reason, leaving her in the nest box she has chosen will likely break the brood. Broodies that are not moved also tend to distract the other hens, and they slow their laying or stop completely.

Our first broody hen was not planned. We had a smaller coop to raise chicks in, but it was full of four-week-old pullets from the feed store. Without another place to put our would-be mother, I used rabbit wire to divide the space. To reduce stress on our mother hen, everything I read strongly suggested she be moved to her new home at night. At 11:00 p.m. one Sunday night, I scooped up the hen with both hands as my wife delicately gathered the ten eggs the hen had been sitting on. Colored brown, blue-green, and white because they were from several breeds of chickens, this was our first clue that this hen was

Mother hens are very nervous about their chicks, but just like human children, these babies quickly learn to run on their own and want to explore the whole world. When they wander too far away, the mother will scold them sharply—but just like human parents, sometimes the chicks obey, and sometimes they don't.

not only hatching out her own egg progeny, but the offspring of many of our other hens too.

My wife put the eggs into a carton for the twenty-foot journey to their new home. Earlier in the afternoon, I had dug a hole to make a ground-level nest so the chicks, when just hatched, couldn't fall out when practicing walking—another caution I'd found in my reading. Charmayne placed the eggs in a single layer on the hay that lined the nest, and I laid our mama hen on top. The hen seemed mildly irritated, but mostly sleepy.

Broody hens take twenty days to hatch out eggs, we have found. I've been told that machine-incubated eggs take an extra day, for whatever reason.

Another mistake I made with our first broody hen was not "candling" the eggs. This is usually done about a week or ten days after the brood begins, using a flashlight at night to see if a chick is developing inside. Not all eggs are viable, and dead eggs begin to rot under the heat of the mother hen, forming gases that can explode the shell, coating the nest, hen, and surrounding eggs with stinky goo. This goo can suffocate the living eggs.

Three days before our chicks were due to hatch out, I brought the broody hen a cup of grain and instead of waiting for me to leave, she jumped off the nest to gobble the food. I took the chance to inspect the nest, to find only nine eggs. The tenth had exploded, and several surrounding eggs were partially coated with hardened goo. We could only wait to see how many would hatch.

"Crazy day!" reads my journal entry on July 31, 2007. "Just after midnight, I went to check out the hen and saw a broken egg just outside her nest." At first, I thought one of the store-bought chicks, who'd escaped from their half of the coop and adopted the mother hen, had broken the egg hours before it was due to hatch. But then I heard peeping.

"Using a stick, I slowly coaxed the mother away from her nest to find one barred Plymouth Rock chick, tiny, fluffy and colored like newly refined gold," I wrote in my journal. "Another egg had a line pecked across its center, and I could see the wet, black feathers of the barred Plymouth Rock chick inside. I was so excited that I told the broody hen thank you out loud and jumped up and did a little dance in the dark."

The next morning, the second chick was out of its shell, its glossy black feathers dry and fluffy, a far cry from the cramped wet bird of hours before. The next morning a third chick had been born, another golden buff Orpington. That day, the hen scattered her nest and the remaining unhatched eggs, only to re-form the nest before dusk, gathering the eggs to sit on them again.

"We'll see what happens," I wrote in my journal that night.

The next morning, August 3, I went out to find a fourth chick had just hatched out of the shell moments before. Feathers still wet, it was struggling to learn to walk, taking half a step and toppling over. Speaking plainly, it was adorable to watch. Every day of the experience, I had felt a depth of awe and privilege that is difficult to put into words.

The next day, I found the last of the eggs in the broody hen's nest had been pecked open, revealing fully formed, dead chicks inside—a stark reminder of the fragile nature of bringing forth generations, and the price of re-creating from scratch knowledge that was once common.

From ten eggs, we had gotten four beautiful new birds.

Notes

1. Gorman, Bjerklie, and Park, "Playing Chicken with Our Antibiotics," 21 Jan. 2002.
2. "More Great News," *Mother Earth News.*

CHAPTER 18

SOLUTIONS FOR THE BACKYARD FLOCK

GATHERING THE HENS

Despite our best efforts, chickens sometimes escape the confines of their coop and range—a child or visitor opens a gate or door; or a loose dog, hawk, or raccoon frighten a chicken into leaping a fence. Or the chickens just get bored and decide to sneak through a hole to scratch around in new territory. Getting the chickens back to where they are supposed to be can be futile, unless you teach your chickens to come when called.

Chickens can learn to gather when prompted by a certain noise. For me, I've trained my chickens to come running when they hear the sound of grain being shaken in a jar. This training is easy, since I use a glass canning jar to measure out food out of a lidded plastic garbage pail every day. I started training the chickens to respond to this sound after the four-year-old at our house began leaving the pasture gate open, letting all the chickens into the yard and garden. When they see the gate open, they run to get out—and pretty soon they're on the road or

The backyard flock sifts through the remains of the horse's hay, searching for anything that might look good to eat.

in the neighbors' yards. I wearied of having chicken rodeos. First, we tried to catch loose chickens by throwing a sheet over them, and then we bought a butterfly net. Neither worked well at all.

Surprisingly, the chickens learned their "call to home" very quickly. And having a Pavlovian prompt to bring them all back to where I want them has greatly simplified life with a curious, animal-loving, four-year-old boy.

ROOSTERS: TO HAVE OR NOT TO HAVE, THAT IS THE QUESTION

The answer lies first in your local law. If you live in a residential non-rural area, your city may allow hens but is unlikely to allow roosters because they are considered too noisy. (We won't go into the debate of why dogs that bark all night get no such treatment—and don't get me wrong, we have a dog. And a cat. And a horse. And a rabbit).

As of this writing, we have a dozen chickens, two of which are roosters, both hatched out on our property three years ago. At one point last year we had thirty-two chickens, eight of which were adult roosters if memory serves me correctly. Now, in

There are pros and cons to having roosters. If roosters are legal in your area, consider your goals. For free-range hens, roosters have many benefits.

The author's grandson, Xander Buckner-Bury, stands barefoot in the pasture surrounded by chickens. Xander has helped gather eggs—and insisted on carrying at least one himself—since before he could walk.

addition to our flock of a dozen, we have a well-stocked freezer. Just being honest.

If you live in a place where roosters are legal, here are some considerations:

Cons of Having a Rooster

- They can be mean. My wife was traumatized in childhood by a rooster that jumped on her. To be fair, we've never had this problem at our house with any of our roosters, ever. And I know why—our four-year-old grandson, who has lived with us since he was born. Speaking frankly, he's dominated the roosters. Our grandson has literally established himself as the alpha male of the flock. Xander has no fear of the roosters or chickens, and never has. He's chased them around the pasture since he was able to run. He's thrown apples and corncobs at them, despite my best efforts to keep a lid on him. The roosters know he's in charge—not only does he never back down if they come skidding up, wings open in a territorial display, he relishes this. He thinks it's a great game and charges right at the roosters. And the roosters turn tail and run away long before he gets anywhere even close to them. Not that the rest of us have ever cowered in front of a rooster. My wife and I make a point of standing our ground and giving the roosters a good scare now and then. And we have excellently behaved roosters to show for it.

• They are up before dawn, crowing. If something startles them in the night, they have been known to crow all night. We have quadruple-paned windows that are very good at deadening the sound, so this has never affected us. Our neighbors have never complained, but to be fair, they have their own hens and roosters, horses, mules, ducks, goats, rabbits, dogs, and cats. We live on a residential street with a minimum of one acre-lot sizes, all with animal rights. We're just that kind of street. If the noise of a rooster is going to bother you and your neighbors, you should probably forego roosters.

• They eat more than any hen, and produce no eggs.

• How shall I put this delicately? They take full advantage of their male role, often in a manner that may seem violent to humans (but is quite normal for chickens). They jump on top of a hen, who is often noisily trying to escape, they use one foot to push the hen's head the ground, the other to clutch the hen's "saddle" feathers, and do their natural-born duty. They do this a lot—and I mean *a lot*. If you see hens with a bald spot on their saddle (their back), don't be alarmed—it's just a sign that there's been a lot of chicken hanky-panky going on. Be prepared: children will want an explanation for all this violence, squawking and, ahem, action.

• If you have two or more roosters, one will be the alpha male. This is easy to tell because the alpha is always the largest. If any other rooster tries to

Three fluffy chicks are herded by their mother. She slowly teaches them the ways of the free-range life, always on the lookout for danger.

mate with the hens, this rooster will fight them. So expect fighting. If there are just two roosters, the alpha may even try to starve the competitor to death by relentlessly chasing him away from food. This is less of an issue if you have a pastured flock. I would not recommend keeping two or more roosters in a confined space.

Pros of Having a Rooster (or more)

• They will defend the hens to their death. This instinct comes in very handy when a snake, raccoon, weasel, mink, or other predator manages to get into the coop at night, or a hawk or rogue dog tries to take a hen or chick in the daytime. Such valiance has cost a couple of roosters their lives at our house but has saved many hens.

• They shepherd the flock. Free-range hens with no roosters have a terrible habit of wandering away, often far away—across the highway, down the street several blocks, into neighbors' yards, and often all these places at once. Roosters don't like their hens to be out of their sight or out of call range at the very least—they are very territorial about this. They keep the hens fairly well accounted for and present, night and day.

• Your flock will be self-sustaining. Truly one of the joys of chicken keeping is watching wet chicks hatching out and stumbling to learn to walk. Another joy is also watching the mother take care of their chicks—gathering them under her wings at night, seeing their little heads popping out randomly around her body, herding them around the coop and pasture, calling them (and they obey!), and letting anyone approaching— human, hen, or rooster—know that they will, in no uncertain terms, be coming anywhere near close enough to touch one of her babies. Best yet, the chicks are free, and the mother does all the work of caring for them, and the hens grow up to produce eggs, and the roosters grow up to . . . well, just remember the smell of the Sunday Crock-Pot dinner in winter.

WASTE NOT, WANT NOT (COMMUNITY EDITION)

What to do if you have a rooster you don't want, and what I like to call the "Sunday Crock-Pot Solution" is not happening at your house, no way, no how, never?

There are options.

When we first got chickens, I was totally with you. Harvesting a bird to eat at our house was NGTH— Not. Going. To. Happen. I grew up on a farm, but I had never harvested a chicken before, and I have never seen one harvested. I had no desire, at all.

I knew, however, that I wanted to let our hens naturally hatch out chicks, because I wanted the grandchildren around our house to experience this.

We've hatched out many broods of chickens now, and in almost every case, half the chicks are male, despite all wishful thinking to the contrary. So if you want the experience, even once, of letting a hen naturally hatch out chicks, but you don't want to keep the resulting roosters (in the coop or otherwise), there are solutions. Just be forewarned that none of these end with the rooster retiring in style to spend the rest of their days in leisure at a picture-perfect farm someplace (though if you can arrange that deal, go for it).

Wildlife Rehabilitation Centers

Every state has at least one or more certified centers where wild animals are taken when they are found wounded but alive or abandoned by their mothers. According to federal law, certain protected species, including all raptors, must be healed if possible and released back into the wild. Before a hawk, eagle, or owl, for example, can be set free, they must pass what is called a "kill test." This simply means that they must prove they have the stamina and endurance to catch and eat their natural prey. In my experience, wildlife rehab centers are always short of live animals that can be used for such tests, and are sometimes forced to spend precious funds to buy them. To me, there is no better, more noble use for an unwanted rooster, or hen, for that matter, than to donate them so that a wild animal can pass the final test that stand between them and freedom. If this option is right for you, be sure you contact your local rehab center in advance, explain what you would like to donate, and set an appointment to drop off your live animals. Because of animal noise ordinances, some rehab centers can only accept roosters they can use that day; you may need to be patient and work with the rehab center's schedule, and this could mean keeping your rooster a week or two.

"Wanted/Offered" boards

On the loading dock at our local farm store is a large whiteboard where anyone with an animal for sale, trade, or giveaway can write a small notice. People seeking specific animals can also leave a message. Other stores have corkboard message boards where you can post similar messages. This is a great way to give away a rooster to a family who may be in need and has no qualms about letting your rooster play a delicious, starring role in that family's Sunday Crock-Pot Solution. It is also possible that someone may want a rooster so they can begin having chicks—I once took in a rooster for this very reason, so it does happen. If this option is for you, contact your local farm stores for information.

Freecycle

As explained earlier, freecycle.org is an online service where people in the local community offer free things to people who want them. I've seen many a rooster given away on Freecycle. I've even taken roosters and hens from people giving them away on Freecycle. This is another great way to put food (your rooster) into the hands of needy or provident families who will turn your burden into a blessing. And as with the previous example, there may be families who are wanting a stud rooster, not a dinner bird. Freecycle is a nationwide nonprofit service that charges no fees, ever. The service is organized geographically, grouping nearby people. In my county, there are three Freecycle groups, one for the north end, the south end, and the central area.

TRANSPORTING ROOSTERS AND CHICKENS

An ailing octogenarian in my community needed to find a home for his flock a few years ago because his own health was failing. I offered to take them

and drove to his house to pick them up. I'd never met the man before, and it was clear that he was ill and physically weak, reluctant to give up his flock, and eager that they go to a good home. I'd gone to his house straight from my office and didn't realize until I arrived that I was in my good clothes and had brought no box or container. The man had nothing to give me to put them in, and his physical strength to even accompany me to the coop was quickly waning. I ended up helping this man catch his birds dressed as I was, putting them in the cab of the truck with me, placing a jacket over the birds on the passenger's side floor, and leaning my briefcase against them in hopes that would encourage them to stay put. Amazingly, this worked. I drove twelve miles with the birds, even getting lost in the dark and stopping to ask for directions, and the chickens never moved, even once.

Clearly, that is not the ideal method. A little advance planning on my part would have lowered my blood pressure on the drive home.

Here are tips for moving chickens:

- Catch them at night. Chickens go into an almost coma-like state after sundown. By far the easiest way to catch any chicken or rooster is to go into their coop at night and grab them by the feet. If you have two hands free (and have someone else hold the flashlight), then you can grab the bird in such a way as to hold their wings to their body—this will mean less flapping around, thus riling up the other chickens a little less. When entering the coop, using as little light as possible helps. Light immediately wakes up chickens. I put my fingers over the flashlight so that only little slates or bars of light come out through my fingers. I use this bit of light to make sure I have the right chicken or rooster, and then I grab them.
- Hold them upside down. When the blood rushes to the chicken's head, they immediately calm

down, do much less squirming and flapping, and usually even stop squawking. This means they are less likely to be injured as you carry them.

• Keep them contained. For a car journey, put them in any container—a plastic storage box, a cat or dog carrier—that will allow them plenty of air, safety from being injured, and will contain them so they are not loose. The chicken will be far quieter and calmer if the container is dark inside.

KEEPING THE POULTRY PEACE WITH DOGS, CATS, AND TURKEYS

We have a large dog, a black lab-collie mix. We were careful to introduce her to the chickens, showing them to her at a distance, gradually bringing them into her sight to see how she would respond. For years now she has wandered free among the flock in the pasture, in the garden, and on the lawn. She has never killed a chicken. Twice she has chased them and taken off a few feathers, but both incidents occurred when we as a family were trying to "rodeo" a loose hen from out of the garden. We were chasing the hen with a net, trying to trap her, and both times our dog got excited and decided to help us out. She got an unprecedented scolding each time. (These chicken rodeos happened before I had learned to train my chickens to come on command, as discussed earlier in this chapter.)

Other than those two experiences, our dog has spent many, many hours with the chickens without chasing, barking, or growling. She's been left completely alone with the free-roaming chickens on many days, without ever a scratch on them or missing feathers. (A skiff of feathers on the ground is always a tell-tale sign that something has happened.) On the contrary, I've seen our dog bark to warn the chickens that a loose neighborhood dog had entered our backyard. For the record, we've never had any

dog kill any of our chickens, but we do keep them in a pasture completely fenced with chicken wire.

Our dog is not the exception to canine-poultry relations. I know several other chicken owners whose dogs do the same. So with a bit of care, it is feasible to keep the peace.

As for our cat, she and the chickens are quite chummy. I can't count the number of times I've gone out to gather the eggs and found our cat, Isis, curled up asleep in one of the empty nest boxes, the chickens just completely ignoring her. I've never seen her chase or hiss at the chickens, ever. We did, when we first got chickens, bring a chicken to introduce to her so she'd know we knew the birds were there. Beyond that, we've never done any special training with our cat.

Our horse, Amie, pays no attention at all to the chickens sharing her pasture, except on winter afternoons when I'm trying to feed Amie her special pellet treats for old-age horses. The chickens have taken a liking to these pellets, and they try to steal them from her while she's eating. To defend herself, Amie snorts at them and sways her head a couple of times, but then gives up and just tries to eat faster. I've learned to throw out a bit of wheat or other food to the chickens before I feed Amie, and then horse and chickens eat separately and in peace.

The chickens do regularly drink out of the large goldfish pond in our back lawn, but they have never tried to peck a fish. And our Japanese Harlequin rabbit, Puck, has no direct interaction with the chickens. We have had wild ravens try to steal grain from the chickens occasionally while they were eating, but the roosters generally scare them off. That's my experience, for what it's worth.

One last note: We've never kept turkeys, although I keep meaning to get some. I know of many chicken owners that keep their turkeys right in with their chickens, sharing the same coop, eating the same food, and they report no problems. There are other experienced poultry-keepers, however, who warn that turkeys can develop a disease called blackhead when exposed to chickens or chicken manure. I don't know anything about the disease. There is ongoing debate regarding this issue in the magazines, books, and Internet forums devoted to poultry issues. If you are considering keeping chickens and turkeys together, I suggest doing some research and talk to other poultry-keepers to get their take on the issue.

SICK CHICKENS

We've never had a sick chicken. This is not uncommon with free-range chickens. Most sick chickens are kept in small enclosures without access to range, from what I've heard and read. I did have a chicken once that had some dried manure stuck on her rear end, which can be a sign of constipation or dehydration. I got some gloves, grabbed her, and cleaned her off, removing a few feathers in the process. She never had any trouble again. We've never medicated any chickens for anything, and we've never had any chicken die of unknown causes.

We did once have a mother hen who apparently accidentally trampled two of her chicks to death while trying to keep track of her energetic offspring. The incident was never repeated by any other hens.

THE CHICKEN COMPOST BIN

Most chicken-keepers are also gardeners. Chickens are great composters in the sense that whatever you feed them, they will break it down for you and give it back in the form of rich manure. They don't eat everything—citrus rinds, for example. But they do like to root through things, and this is can be put to use as free compost-pile aeration.

Behind our barn, I've built a large, rustic (euphemism for ugly) compost bin using free pallets. After first building it about sixteen cubic feet, I filled it far faster than I'd imagined, in just a few months, so I had to take it apart and quadruple the size. I installed a chicken-sized entryway in both versions, and since then I've put all daily household chicken scraps into this compost bin. This has been useful in several ways:

- Chicken Cafeteria. When the chickens are let out each morning, they know to head straight for this compost bin, instead of surrounding me and even jumping up to get food out of my hands when I don't give it to them fast enough.
- Free Labor. They scratch and dig in the compost bin, helping to break down the organic matter and oxygenate the pile, allowing greater beneficial aerobic bacterial activity. Our chickens like the compost bin so much that there is always one or two hanging out inside at any time of the day.
- Green Waste Recycling. The compost bin can also be a place to put chicken manure, layered in with garden weeds (before they've gone to seed), corn stalks, yard leaves (and if you are like me, all the yard leaves you can get from neighbors), pine needles, pine cones, and even clean cardboard. Worms love cardboard, and the fiber makes a great soil additive. All printing ink in the U.S. is nontoxic by federal law, and most ink is soy-based. Shiny cardboard or cardboard with tape or glue on it should not be added to the compost pile. Beyond magpies, we've never had any problem with raccoons or other animals being attracted to the pile, but this may be because it is inside our pasture, which is completely fenced with chicken wire. Newsprint that is not glossy could go in the compost bin if weighted down by other materials to keep it from blowing away.
- A Cleaner Chicken Range. To keep the chickens from scattering what's inside the compost bin all over their range area, block the bottom of the

chicken entrance in the compost bin wall with a piece of scrap board about six inches high.

KEEPING EGGSHELLS THICK

When our first chickens began laying eggs, they had wonderfully thick shells that took a real *crack!* to open. This went on for a few months and then one day I picked up an egg to wash it and broke in my hand. Examining the other eggs, I began to notice that the shells were spider-webbed with tiny cracks, much like the eggs from grocery stores. A little research showed that my chickens were calcium deficient. I went to the farm store and purchased a bag of crushed oyster shells, per the recommendation of several books.

Now I know a more self-sufficient way, using an old pioneer trick.

Whenever we use eggs at our house, we crush the shells and add them to the chicken bowl, where they dry. These are thrown into the pasture compost bin with all the other chicken scraps, where the chickens will pick at them as their own internal cravings dictate. This natural method of recycling has worked very well for us for years now. Just be sure to crush the shells and give them a chance to dry out a little. This method is not my invention; it is something that experienced poultry keepers have widely suggested in books and magazines.

This method has side-benefits as well. Any calcium left in the compost bin will end up in the garden, where it benefit's the soil and crops over time.

Take this next bit as you will. Once I had a dream that the world ran short of easily accessible calcium and people were trying to find old landfills to get out all the trillions of eggshells that had been thrown away over generations. Admittedly this was just a strange dream, and the world has no shortage of calcium. But I just feel better knowing that instead of consigning a perfectly good mineral to be sealed in a landfill to stew, I'm re-using what I have. To me, that is provident living.

I will also note that the natural digestion of a chicken relies on grit to process the food in the stomach, which is another reason why factory-farmed chickens without access to the natural landscape must be fed ground grain and small crumbles of granite. Backyard chickens too should be allowed to self-feed on granite crumbles as desired if they do not have access to some portion of land outside the coop. Free-range chickens, as I figured out after wasting money on my first bag of granite crumbles, don't need to be fed small stones because they pick them up themselves while pecking and scratching outside.

WASHING EGGS

Opinions about this vary. After gathering them, I wash my eggs—at least the ones I plan to sell—in plain faucet hot water with a small, freshly laundered dish rag. During the 1960s, when they were selling eggs commercially, my grandparents used some kind of special egg detergent, which they purchased from a local co-operative. I came across a suggestion from a Midwest extension service office one day instructing home egg producers to wash their eggs in water of a certain temperature mixed with bleach. That may be fine for some people, but there is no way I'm bleaching the eggs I feed to our family. And many sources decry washing eggs at all.

Historically, eggs were not washed, because eggs are sealed naturally with a clear protective coating called the bloom that helps them resist drying out. When you first put a fresh egg in water, you can actually feel this coating turn slippery in your hands. I've lost too many eggs to the bottom of the kitchen sink because I was washing too fast, didn't have a good grip, and the slippery bloom helped the egg escape me.

When we first began raising our own eggs, I never used one without washing it first. Now I admit that I use clean, unwashed eggs all the time when cooking. Not, however, for making cookies, because I know my grandkids and I will be eating some of the dough raw—better to be safe than sorry. I never sell an egg that has not been washed, for the same reason.

TIPS FOR WASHING EGGS

- Use the hottest water possible.
- Don't attempt to wash eggs sullied with manure or egg yolk.
- Always use a freshly laundered washcloth.
- Wash promptly. Don't let eggs pile up or sit out on the counter.
- Allow eggs to air dry completely before refrigerating.
- Avoid rubbing eggs dry, as this may crack them.
- After eggs are dry, inspect for stains, discoloration, or spider-web cracks. Avoid selling these eggs.
- Some chicken breeds lay speckled eggs, often light to medium brown eggs with medium to dark speckles. If you are new to poultry keeping, or new to a particular breed, don't confuse naturally speckled eggs with dirty eggs.
- When washing brown eggs, especially medium to dark hues, the natural shell coloring will sometimes rub off onto a clean cloth. This is normal and should not be confused with dirt.

WHAT TO SUSPECT IF YOU FIND DIRTY EGGS

You will get dirty eggs, especially if you don't clean out the nest boxes regularly.

Chickens like to share the same nest box, because chickens naturally group their eggs so that only one hen has to sit on them for three weeks to hatch them. This means that one chicken will go in, lay her egg, leave, the next chicken enters the same box, lays her egg, and so on. If it is rainy or snow, or even if they just stepped in the waterer, the chickens can leave muddy three-pronged footprints on the eggs, which may stain the shells even if washed off.

One reason that I switched from lining the nest boxes with straw to pine shavings was because some of the just-laid eggs would be imprinted with straw stains before the bloom could dry.

On rare occasions, especially if a lack of calcium is causing thin eggs shells, an egg may break when a chicken steps on it. This makes a mess over the nearby eggs.

Sometimes the worst happens—a chicken sullies an egg with manure, either from walking into another chicken's mess just before getting into the nest box, or even just answering the call of nature in the nest box.

SOLUTIONS FOR KEEPING EGGS CLEAN IN THE COOP

- Install a homemade wooden chicken ladder from the ground up to the nest boxes. Chickens will prefer to walk up this ladder instead of jumping or flying up, and the walk will help remove debris from their feet before they enter the nest box.
- Change the lining of the nest boxes often.
- If your chickens are allowed to free-range outside the coop, strategically place the nest boxes on the wall farthest from the coop entrance. This allows chickens to dry their feet off a little when coming in from rain, snow, dew, garden irrigation, lawn sprinklers, or any other source of outdoor water.
- Gather the eggs more often, if possible. The sooner you collect them, the less chance another chicken has to come in and walk on them.

SOLUTIONS FOR UNWANTED EGGS

If eggs are dirty beyond washing, or stained or discolored even after washing, one option is to cook the eggs completely and feed them to the family dog, or to pigs, if you have them. Dogs love the protein content of eggs, and eggs are a healthy option for dogs just as they are for humans. Plus, eggs have been said to increase the gloss of a dog's coat. And pigs will eat anything, even raw eggs.

Misshapen eggs can be a sign of an old age in a hen or illness. And sometimes hens just lay the occasionally odd-shaped egg—pointy, wrinkled, elongated, rippled, or even eggs with wartlike calcium lumps on them. Often these eggs are perfectly edible. Inspect them immediately before use by breaking them into a clean bowl. If anything appears off about the egg, discard the egg. Never eat an egg if you have doubts about its purity.

Last night, when I went to gather our eggs just after dark, one of our Rhode Island Red hens was sleeping in the nest box—a sure sign that she had gone "broody" and decided to begin the three-week process of hatching out chicks. For reasons discussed later, hens sometimes give up a brood after starting the process. If the hen has been sitting on them for more than a day or two, they are likely to be bloody inside at least, and may have chicks in different stages of development. Such eggs should be discarded. This morning, when I went to let our chickens out, my broody Rhode Island Red had already given up on motherhood, leaving behind the three eggs she had been sitting on. Even these should not be used for human consumption, although they could still be opened, inspected, and cooked for the family dog if the contents appear normal.

If you've been on vacation or out of town for a few days and were unable to gather the eggs, cook the eggs for the dog. If you have a lot of these eggs (we had twenty waiting for us after being gone for three days for a funeral recently), then crack the eggs into sandwich bags, putting one doggie-meal's worth into one bag, and freeze them for the dog later. Frozen eggs can be thawed at room temperature or in water. Cook immediately upon thawing.

When hens sit in a community nest—eggs laid in the same nest that day by other hens—to add her own egg, the hen often bury those eggs within her feathers to cushion them. Sometimes these eggs can be buried deeply or even tucked in folds of skin or between the legs and the body. If the chicken gets off the nest suddenly—because you have just opened the door to feed them or let them out to range for the day, for example—the egg may not work its way out of the feathers for several steps or more. These eggs can sometimes be found on the coop floor, or outside the coop door. Because they have been on the ground, the safest bet is to feed them to the family dog, pig, or discard them.

The elderly widow woman who lived next door

The author's family horse, Amie, one of the most gentle creatures on earth. In this photo, she is surrounded by the first irrigation water of spring.

to my grandmother came by every week for many years to take away any cracked, stained, or otherwise unsellable eggs that my grandmother might have. My grandmother wanted to get rid of them, and the free eggs were priced right for this humble widow woman. I wouldn't advocate trying to pawn off your cracked, discolored eggs on a neighbor, but if you are not selling your eggs and you know of a family in need, offer them your extra (perfect) eggs free of charge.

If your in the mood for a moment of levity, let the grandkids pitch the eggs against the house, like my grandmother used to do, or at some target in a location where you don't mind splattered eggs or can immediately wash off the residue. If egg pitching is not an old-fashioned game, I don't know what is!

VACATIONING AWAY FROM YOUR BARNYARD ANIMALS

When friends of ours recently moved onto a five-acre property and decided to get their first chickens, they were anxious to know what on earth we do with all our animals when we go on vacation. We are a vacationing family and travel all over the world. With a few guidelines, you can leave your animals behind worry free.

Horses

Keep a large enough water trough to supply several weeks of water in summer without refilling. If your pasture is green and plentiful, horses will feed themselves. In winter, an electric de-icer can be used. A reliable friend or neighbor should be asked to feed hay.

Chickens

For short vacations in summer, leave the coop door open and allow the hens to free-range. This does risk a predator entering at night, but if you have a long habit of keep the chickens locked up and a well-fenced chicken run or range, predators are generally far less likely to attack in the night during summer as compared to winter. A large trough of water with edges chickens can perch to reach the water works well. Our chickens are self-watered from the horse trough all summer long. For longer summer vacations, or in winter, place a fifty-pound bag (or more as necessary) in a self-feeder inside the coop and keep the chickens locked inside with an electric waterer if temperatures are below freezing, or a regular water if not. Be sure the waterer is large enough to keep the chickens supplied in your absence.

Rabbits

A self-feeding supply of hay pellets, free access to water, and a secure, shaded cage are all a rabbit needs.

Fish

For kicks, let me add this tip. If you have indoor aquarium fish and you need to leave on vacation, put large aquarium rocks inside the tank and let them grow algae on them. Feed them well just before leaving, and the fish will feed themselves off the rocks while you are gone.

Other

We don't keep goats, cows, llamas, donkeys, sheep, pigs, or other barnyard animals. If you need vacation tips for these animals, consult a neighbor with first-hand knowledge—or just hire their teenager to feed and keep an eye on them while your gone.

KEEPING A POULTRY JOURNAL

"Woke to two pullets gone, taken by a predator who dug a hole under the coop on the east side. The

Chicks, like children, grow up surprisingly fast. Chicks like these are always a huge hit when taken to school (with lots of supervision) for show-and-tell.

chicks were a buff Orpington and a barred Rock."
—journal, July 27, 2007

Keeping a journal of my chickens may be the best poultry-keeping decision I ever made. It is a working database of egg counts, broody hens, harvested animals, and predator deaths. I have pages of notes about successes and failures. Best of all, there is one place where I can document everything about my flock, including information about disease and treatments, natural deaths, egg counts, odd eggs, eating habits, experimental feed, broodiness, first eggs, roosting for the first time, and even such things as temperatures or when the coops were built or equipment added. Here are tips for preserving your own poultry experiences on paper:

Take photos

The hens and roosters in my coop are all adults, but memories rush back when I look at photos of them as chicks, playing with my grandsons. I once took photos only for fun, but today I try to document our chickens every month or two. Beside offering a comprehensive visual record, it's just fun! If you are not inclined to write, a journal of photos is an easy way to keep records of egg counts and colors, your coop system, feeding, harvesting, and poultry health.

Go with short and simple

Over the years, I have found that I rarely need to write more than a few sentences on any given day. Short entries do the trick.

Jot down what works—and what doesn't

My notes from June 2007 include these: "I got chicks from Intermountain Farmers—assorted bantams, buff Orpingtons, and barred Rocks. We put them in the 'chick' coop and something killed four of them overnight. I sandbagged the coop and bought four more and two more were killed the next night so I've been posting (our dog) Sharky out there every night and no more dead chicks! Getting the chicks this late worked well because it was hot enough for them to stay outside even the first night, instead of in the house."

Make it yours

I keep a personal journal, but that doesn't mean my poultry journal is without personal experiences. Looking back, the personal entries are the most fun to read. For example: "Feb. 3, 2006: Manny (our son-in-law) killed a rooster. Charmayne cooked it." And May 14, 2006: "I forgot to plant the tomatoes, which I bought yesterday at Intermountain Farmers Association, of all places, while picking up feed corn for the chickens."

Sketch in details

While it's true that rough drawings add visual interest, a quick illustration now and then also helps document your poultry history. For example, on the night our first-ever broody hen's eggs began hatching out, I sketched the line one chick had pecked across the exact center of the egg. If you are artistic, put in a few quick watercolor studies of your chickens or even their tracks in the mud of your backyard pond.

Specifics count

A garden journal is a repository for years of experience that would otherwise be lost to time. I can jot notes on what feeds I'm using, when feed is switched seasonally, how I've dealt with predators, the consumption rate of additives such as oyster shells or granite pebbles. I can track food prices over time, allowing me to figure my cost per egg or animal harvested if I wish. If you have a mobile coop, you can document where it's been and for how long. If your coops are stationary like mine, you can track when they were last cleaned. The poultry journal is also a great place to catalog anything new you've learned from others with chicken-keeping experience or information gleaned from books or articles worth remembering for future reference.

Preserve the homestead heritage

The last generation with significant poultry-keeping experience in America is the World War II generation, whose members grow more sparse with each passing day. I am convinced that keeping notes on our chickens may be more than a hobby—it may help save our heritage. More people are coming to lament the knowledge, breeds, and wisdom won through experience that we have already lost. My grandfather, Phill Nielson, kept a farm diary every day of his working life, cataloging simple information that now not only represents my heritage but is a working history of an age gone by, knowledge that could never be re-created had it not been recorded in his hand. A poultry journal is a place to catalog the heritage information future generations may need, whether because of a need to return to the land or simply because they want to. And it can be an unusual conversation piece or family history item that may spur the interest of the rising generation.

Keep a combination garden/poultry journal

Branch out. It's not just the chickens that benefit from having a written record over time. Expanding your poultry journal to include garden activity allows you to catalog not only the first spring egg but also the first crocuses or when your Veronica geraniums got sunburnt. You can also record maps of your garden plot from year to year to guide your crop rotation, and even press a fall leaf or three.

Avoid journal guilt

There are whole seasons missing from my poultry journal, and that's okay. Sometimes I'm not in the mood, and at the busiest times, weeks go by without entries. For me, the journal is good enough if I write when I can.

Do it with joy

Whether in the barnyard, my poultry journal, my marriage, or my career, I try to remember that if I'm not enjoying myself, I'm not doing it right. I keep a poultry journal so I can look back on what I've accomplished, catalog my ideas, successes and photos in one place, and have a tangible chart of my personal and poultry progress. Happy chicken journaling!

CHOOSING THE RIGHT BREEDS FOR YOU

Not all chicken breeds are good winter layers. If your primary goal is to provide eggs for your family, be sure you choose the best year-round laying breeds. Some breeds were developed over time because of their excellent meat, some for their capacity for producing eggs, and some for their ability to produce eggs well for a year or two and then still be a good bird to harvest for meat. Other breeds are valued simply for their unusual coloring or plumage, or even just their capacity for producing colored or speckled eggs. If you have specific goals, take the time to research which breeds are best suited for helping you meet your goals.

As previously discussed, some breeds fare better in bitter winter temperatures than others. Choose breeds best suited to the conditions you can provide. Bantam hens are a class of chicken developed to be a sort of diminutive or dwarf version of many standard breeds. The advantage of bantams is that they eat less and are thus cheaper to feed over their lifetime. Many people also like their size. Bantams produce eggs that are small to medium sized, as opposed to standard

(left) A hen looks out of an enclosure in winter. The author's hens are provided with several bales of straw in a roofed area to scratch in during the worst of winter, when temperatures don't rise above freezing for weeks at a time and deep snow covers the pasture where the chickens normally range.

(right) A "Buff Orpington" hen looks idyllic in the light of sunset, surrounded by wildflowers in the pasture. But if you look closely, you can see the bare patch of skin on her "saddle" (back) where the feathers have been worn off because she has been "mounted" so many times by the rooster. Whether this means she is having a great life or not is up to you, the reader, to decide!

breeds which should normally produce large to extra-large eggs.

Some breeds are considered to make better pets, some are believed to be more child friendly, produce less territorial roosters, or birds perhaps less prone to certain disease or conditions. Some breeds make excellent mothers, and some are unlikely to ever sit on a nest long enough to hatch out chicks. A breed-by-breed comparison is beyond the scope of this book, but several are already available in other books and on the Internet. Seek out poultry keepers in your area; many are happy to show off their flock to visitors and discuss their experiences and advice.

CHAPTER 19

"MUSEUM EGGS"

MODERN EGG-KEEPING

The pioneers used several methods for storing excess eggs for leaner months. The best option, though, is not a pioneer method, and that is freezing. To freeze eggs, crack them into freezer bag and then put the bags in the freezer. Bagging them individually or in pairs will make them more convenient for later use—don't try to put a dozen eggs in a bag and then expect to chip off a single egg for baking a month later. I've successfully used eggs frozen for more than a year. Frozen eggs are best for baking, as they will be a little watery and less solid when thawed. If you are freezing dirty or old eggs to feed your family dog, be careful to mark which eggs are for the family and which are for the family pet. Having a few eggs in the freezer is never a bad idea—ours get used most often on a Sunday afternoon when someone wants to make brownies or lemon bars, and we've just used the last fresh egg in the house.

Water Glass Eggs

My wife remembers when her grandmother stored some of the summer bounty of eggs in "water glass" for winter use. As a girl she used to dread being asked to slip her hand into the cool, gelatin-like goo to retrieve an egg or two. The chemical name for water glass is sodium silicate, which can be purchased at drug stores and mixed with water to create a clear, viscous solution for storing eggs. Eggs in water glass are kept in the cellar in a covered crock or jar, or at least out of sunlight in a cool place. I've never tried using water glass, but it could be a fun experiment. My wife, on the other hand, has no desire to relive this part of her childhood.

Buttered Eggs

I've read several accounts of an old Irish technique of storing eggs by taking hot eggs straight from the hen and rubbing them with buttered hands to seal them. This was supposed to keep them for several months, and be a higher quality stored egg than so-called "cooking eggs." Several sources report that buttered eggs are still sold today as a specialty in the historic market in Cork, Ireland. I tried this at home once, but the hen pecked at me when I tried to get the egg and I halfheartedly gave up.

Cooking Eggs

Before the modern era, eggs were sold either fresh eggs or cooking eggs. The latter were storage eggs, usually taken from the summer excess and stored until the leaner times of winter. Because these eggs were old, they were watery or ribbony (from desiccation) when cracked open and thus were deemed best for baking.

Ice House Eggs

In the pioneer days of Leamington and Lynndyl, Utah, where I later grew up, winter was the time for cutting blocks of ice from the Sevier River. The men lifted them with huge iron tongs, loaded them on wagons, and sold the ice door-to-door. The ice was packed into individual icehouses in a thick layer of sawdust, where it would keep most of the summer if well managed. According to my grandparents, excess eggs were sometimes stored in the sawdust, as well as containers of milk and other homemade items. My grandmother recalled that sometimes eggs would get lost in the sawdust, or you would search the sawdust hoping to find an egg in a moment of need.

"MUSEUM EGGS"

A flawless egg, if left alone for years, will become hollow, the water inside slowly leaving out the six thousand pores that dot its surface, the remnant fading to dust inside the shell. Such an egg gives off no trace of stench.

Few people know this anymore. There was once, in pre-industrial Ukraine, a thriving folk art dedicated to the elaborate decoration of such museum-quality eggs. I still have a few I did myself years ago. In the United States this art of drying whole eggs for display is now rarely heard of—factory farm eggs are often so thin-shelled and riddled with hairline cracks that they stink and even burst if dried.

In my own way, I've decided to revive the practice.

I work as a journalist, and my newspaper once ran a story about a local family, clearly new to raising chickens, who genuinely believed their hen had laid the largest egg in the world. The article reported their quest to have the egg certified as such. When I read the article, I was gently amused. With so many of us far removed from the source of our food, we have come to believe eggs surely must always be as we find them in the store—uniform, matching, predictable.

In the barnyard, chickens lay a never-ending spectacle of curious and rude eggs, ranging from enormous to miniscule, slumped, bent, dented, deeply wrinkled, sharply pointed, elongated, double-yokers, egg-white only, warted by calcium deposits, eggs within eggs (shell and all), and paper eggs—a hen's first attempt, with a fragile, paper-thin shell.

Of these, only the most exactingly uniform specimens make it onto store shelves. The rest are turned into powdered eggs or packaged bulk eggs (without shells) for commercial bakeries. I've heard of egg producers selling these imperfect eggs by the dozen at the factory store for cut-rate prices. For the home egg producer, all these odd eggs—remember when that term described someone one-off from everyone else?—are simply part of the day-to-day supply. If you sell eggs, as we do, these odd eggs often become the family eggs, leaving the public-ready eggs for those who put cash on the counter.

For years we've paused to marvel at the oddest eggs to come from our coop. Then we crack and used them, just as all the others. But after reading the article about this local family and their "world's largest" egg, I decided to start a collection of my own "museum eggs." I've been taking the very strangest eggs and putting them in bowls on a high shelf to slowly dry out. I vaguely envision them become as some kind of educational tool, bringing children and their parents back to a knowledge of what eggs—everyday eggs—look like.

At any rate, they are a curiosity and conversation piece.

From the *Boston Cooking-school Cook Book*, Fannie Merritt Farmer, 1918

Eggs, like milk, form a typical food, inasmuch as they contain all the elements, in the right proportion, necessary for the support of the body. Their highly concentrated, nutritive value renders it necessary to use them in combination with other foods rich in starch (bread, potatoes, etc.). In order that the stomach may have enough to act upon, a certain amount of bulk must be furnished.

A pound of eggs (nine) is equivalent in nutritive value to a pound of beef. From this it may be seen that eggs, at even twenty-five cents per dozen, should not be freely used by the strict economist. Eggs being rich in protein serve as a valuable substitute for meat. In most families, their use in the making of cake, custard, puddings, etc., renders them almost indispensable. It is surprising how many intelligent women, who look well to the affairs of the kitchen, are satisfied to use what are termed "cooking eggs"; this shows poor judgment from an economical standpoint. Strictly fresh eggs should always be used if obtainable. An egg after the first twenty-four hours steadily deteriorates. If exposed to air, owing to the porous structure of the shell, there is an evaporation of water, air rushes in, and decomposition takes place.

White of egg contains albumen in its purest form. Albumen coagulates at a temperature of from 134° to 160° F. Herein lies the importance of cooking eggs at a low temperature, thus rendering them easy of digestion. Eggs cooked in boiling water are tough and horny, difficult of digestion, and should never be served.

When eggs come from the market, they should be washed, and put away in a cold place.

Ways of Determining Freshness of Eggs.
I. Hold in front of candle flame in dark room, and the centre should look clear.
II. Place in basin of cold water, and they should sink.
III. Place large end to the cheek, and a warmth should be felt.

Ways of Keeping Eggs.
I. Pack in sawdust, small end down.
II. Keep in lime water.
III. From July to September a large number of eggs are packed, small ends down in cases having compartments, one for each egg, and kept in cold storage. Eggs are often kept in cold storage six months, and then sold as cooking eggs.

These are not my first museum eggs. There is another, two decades old, prized among my most meaningful possessions. It is the last egg ever taken from my grandparents' coop in Lynndyl. I came to own it by serendipity.

One bright Sunday afternoon, while telling my grandparents in Lynndyl about our backyard flock, my grandfather offered us anything we might find useful from his nearly seventy-year-old coop.

Entering the long-unused building, we dug from the decades of mess and dust a chicken grain feeder and a bank of zinc nest boxes. Over the two-hour drive home, the wind blew the dust across the highway.

Unloading the truck the next day, I found the wind had cleared away enough old muck to partially reveal a desiccated, unbroken egg.

Today as then, this egg is numinous to me, a

chance to touch a dimming family history before it recedes from living memory.

Great-grandma Lexia has been gone many years, and her coop long since torn down. My Sigurd, Utah, grandparents are buried in the red clay, a ton-weight river stone marking their grave. Grandpa Nielson is buried on the Lynndyl farm, the old corn patch turned into a cemetery. Grandma Nielson alone remains, fighting a mind bent on denying her short-term memory—our family history, however, she knows lucidly. I take my grandsons to our own coop to gather eggs so that in time, they will have some link in memory to these, my ancestors they will never know.

CHAPTER 20

FORGOTTEN RECIPES

EASY PIONEER YEAST PANCAKES

(4 minutes total preparation)

The night before you want to have pancakes for breakfast, mix into a quart jar:

- ¾ cup warm water
- ¾ cup flour (I use fresh-ground whole wheat)
- 1 Tbsp. pioneer yeast

Tighten lid loosely and leave overnight. In the morning, in a medium mixing bowl, whisk together:

- 2 eggs
- 1 Tbsp. olive oil
- ¼ cup milk
- ¼ tsp. salt

Add the yeast mixture into the egg mixture. Using a spatula (do not use a whisk) gently fold ingredients together until just incorporated. Cook as usual. Enjoy!

CHARMAYNE'S GOLDEN PEACH SAUCE

This irresistible recipe is a long-time family favorite at our house.

Puree in a blender, or mash by hand:

- 1 quart home-canned peaches

Heat in saucepan over the stove until warm. Serve over pancakes, waffles, or crepes. For a thicker sauce, drain some peach juice from the bottle before blending. Bottled pears, apricots, or other fruit may be substituted for peaches. This recipe has historically been made with the oldest bottles of peaches from the previous year, in which the peaches exposed to air space at the top of the jar are just beginning to discolor due to oxidation over time. In our house, we still use this recipe for this purpose. Before using any jar of home-canned fruit, ensure the seal has remained intact during storage.

HEARTY PIONEER-YEAST LOAVES

Makes two loaves. I use whole wheat flour ground fresh at home to make this recipe, but white flour or half-white, half-whole wheat will also work. Using bread flour will result in the lightest loaf. (In the rest and raising periods in this recipe, I found the best success by turning the oven onto preheat at 350 degrees for 20 seconds, turning off the oven, and placing the dough inside. During the long rising period, I repeated this 20-second warming at the half-way point).

Into a large bowl, add;
- 3 cups pioneer yeast starter
- 4 cups flour
- 2 tsp. salt
- 2 cup room temperature water

Step One: With a wooden paddle or spoon (or KitchenAid or Bosch mixer), combine ingredients until the resulting wet dough is thick and elastic, about five minutes. Let dough rest in a warm spot for five minutes.

Add: ½ cup flour at a time (kneading until dough is no longer sticky)

This step is likely to require quite a bit of flour, perhaps three cups or more. Knead for a total of about 8 to 10 minutes, until the dough becomes a smooth ball.

Step Two: Allow dough to rise 3 to 4 hours, until doubled in size, occasionally sprinkling a few drops of water over the top of the dough to keep the surface moist, if necessary.

Step Three: Divide the dough in half, shape into loaves, and place in buttered, floured loaf pans. Allow dough to rise until doubled, about 90 minutes. Bake for 30–40 minutes at 350 degrees. For a crunchier crust, bake at 450 degrees for 10 minutes, then reduce temperature to 350 degrees for 20–30 minutes. Serve hot with butter and preserves.

For scones:

Follow steps one and two above. After the dough has doubled in size, heat oil in a deep pan. (I use olive oil, which smokes a bit more than other oils but is healthier). Cutting off pieces of dough, form scones by hand. Fry until golden brown on both sides, and serve.

For breadsticks:

(Makes two cookie sheets of bread sticks; for one cookie sheet, halve the ingredients in step one.) Follow steps one and two above. After the dough has doubled in size, punch it down, divide in half, and roll out to fill two cookie sheets (use a cookie sheet with raised edges). Allow dough to rise in cookie sheets until doubled in size, about 90 minutes. Pour evenly over the dough:

- ¾ cube melted butter

Spread the melted butter with a spatula if necessary to cover the entire surface of the dough. Using a pizza cutting wheel, and without removing dough from cookie sheet, run the cutter up and down to cut dough into strips. Sprinkle over the cut strips:

- 1 cup grated Parmesan cheese

Bake in a 350 degree oven for 10–13 minutes, until dough just barely begins to brown. Remove and serve.

This loaf of whole-wheat bread was made using pioneer yeast. Pioneer yeast is only sour if you want it to be (and this loaf is not).

For pizza dough:

(Makes four pizza crusts. For two crusts, halve the ingredients in step one.) Follow steps one and two. After the dough has doubled in size, punch it down. Divide dough into four equal balls. Roll out each ball and place on pizza trays. Top with desired sauce and toppings. Bake in oven at 375 degrees for 10–12 minutes.

SUCCULENT SLOW-ROASTED VEGETABLES

This is one of my all-time winter favorites.

In a glass baking dish, combine root vegetables rough-chopped to approximately uniform chunks. Drizzle with olive oil and stir to coat. Top to taste with fresh or dried herbs, including rosemary, thyme, sage, marjoram, caraway, or parsley. Chopped garlic, white and black pepper, and sea salt also add favor.

Chopped vegetable, as available:
- Potatoes
- Carrots
- Onions
- Cabbage chunks
- brussels sprouts (whole)
- Kohlrabi
- Turnips
- Beets

Carrots, onions, beets, potatoes, and turnips are topped with crisp bacon to make roasted winter vegetables for Sunday dinner.

- Rutabaga
- Summer squash (in larger chunks, or add halfway through cooking)
- Winter squash and pumpkin
- Parsnips
- Eggplant (in larger chunks or add halfway through cooking)
- Whole, small tomatoes (add halfway through cooking)

Bake at 375 degrees for 60 minutes or until vegetables are easily speared with a fork. Drizzle with melted butter and serve hot.

12-MONTH GARDEN OMELET BAR

If you have your own eggs, or just your own garden produce, a family omelet buffet is a great supper or lunch idea. Simply lay out omelet fillings as available. Each family member chooses their own fillings; one person generally cooks the omelets, one at a time. Follow any basic omelet recipe. I'm partial to Julia Child's recipe in *Mastering the Art of French Cooking*.

Omelet fillings, as available:
- Grated cheese: Parmesan, swiss, cheddar, asiago, havarti, many others
- Garden fresh, grated: potato, carrot, beet, turnip, squash, any root vegetable
- Chopped greens: collards, kale, chard, beet tops, green onions, kohlrabi tops, bok choi, Chinese cabbage, spinach, mache (corn salad)
- Chopped: onions, broccoli, raab, asparagus, tomatoes, cabbage, green beans, brussel sprouts, mushrooms, peppers
- Peas, chickpeas, or cooked wheatnuts, barley, quinoa, or rice

A sprinkling of flax meal (rich in omega-3 fatty acids) Herbs or spices as desired. I recommend oregano, chives, basil, tumeric, white and black pepper, salt. Pre-cooked proteins: sweet Italian sausage, breakfast sausage, Polish sausage, crisp bacon, chopped ham, shredded chicken or turkey, pepperoni, or Canadian bacon

Omelets are one of the author's favorite self-sufficient foods. This one was made using backyard eggs and grated winter carrots, Swiss chard, onion, and grated beet, all picked fresh from the winter garden in February.

SIMPLE WINTER GREENS WITH KALE

Another favorite kale recipe.

Into salted, boiling water, drop:
- ¾ cup (per person) fresh chopped kale (or mixed greens as available)

Boil for one minute; remove greens with ladle and plunge into ice water. Ladle from ice water and immediately sauté in a frying pan with butter and a touch of olive oil for 30 seconds or so; squeeze lemon or lime juice over the top, and a dash of balsamic vinegar and sauté for another ten seconds or so. Enjoy.

PIONEER PAN TOAST

My grandmother in Lynndyl, Utah, made this countless times, and I loved it every time.

Place in a skillet over medium heat:
- Buttered, sliced bread (I prefer homemade whole wheat)

Toast on just one side until sizzling and golden brown. May be served with a fried egg or breakfast sausage, or as a side dish at supper. Toppings include garlic powder, fruit preserves, or cinnamon-sugar. I like to eat mine with my fried egg topped with Parmesan cheese.

HANDMADE RUSTIC RAVIOLI

This ravioli is made with sweet Italian sausage and dandelion greens, but other greens and protein may be used instead. This rustic recipe uses one-half of a cracked egg shell as the measure for the water needed—a truly ancient technique. This is designed purposefully to make enough ravioli to feed four people, with enough left over to freeze for a later meal.

Ravioli Filling
- 1 pound sweet Italian sausage
- ½ bushel (about two large salad bowls) dandelion greens and crowns
- 1 cup grated raw carrot
- 1 cup grated raw beet

Gather a half bushel (about two large salad bowls) of dandelion greens and crowns from your garden or property. Dandelion crowns are the pale-to-white, tightly packed leaves immediately above the root. Never eat dandelions that may have been exposed to any herbicides or pesticides, even treatments that may have drifted from neighboring properties. I use a garden shovel to cut whole dandelion heads just below the ground.

In the kitchen, bring a large pot of water to a boil. Meanwhile, thoroughly wash greens and crowns, removing any roots. Rough-chop the greens and finely chop the crowns. Submerge greens and crowns, carrot, and beet into boiling water. Boil until greens are wilted, 1–2 minutes. Drain completely.

In a bowl, add to the drained greens:
- 1 beaten egg
- 2 cups Parmesan cheese (or other cheese by preference)

The egg will help bind the mix together for spooning onto the dough.

Pasta Dough

STEP ONE:

Combine:

- 2¼ cups flour (I use whole wheat)
- 1 tsp. salt
- 1 tsp. baking powder

Add to dry mix:

- 3 eggs
- 3 half egg shells of water

Knead dough until stiff, 2–3 minutes. Divide in quarters. On a well-floured surface, roll one quarter until dough resembles thick paper, being careful not to let the dough rip.

STEP TWO:

In a bowl, beat:

- 2 eggs

Use beaten eggs to thinly but completely coat the rolled out dough quarter, reserving remaining egg mixture for remaining dough quarters. Dot the dough with quarter-sized tablespoons of ravioli filling, keeping an inch and a half between any two spoonfuls. No filling should be placed closer than one-half inch from the border of the dough.

Roll out another quarter of dough to resemble thick paper. Place this dough over the first dough. Using two fingers, carefully pat the dough layers together, creating pockets of filling. Use a pizza cutter to roughly cut out each individual ravioli pocket. Taking each ravioli one at a time, press the edges together to ensure a good seal.

STEP THREE:

Bring a large pot of water to a rapid boil. Meanwhile, using the remaining two quarters of dough, repeat the process outlined in step two.

STEP FOUR:

Boil fresh ravioli for 1–2 minutes. Remove from pot, drain, and serve with melted butter and Parmesan cheese, or marinara sauce or Alfredo sauce.

STEP FIVE:

Freeze remaining ravioli by placing them in a single layer on wax paper on a cookie sheet (may also be frozen on dinner plates with wax paper). Freeze for 24 hours and then transfer to freezer bags.

HUNGER GAP OMELETS WITH WINTER KALE

One of my favorite winter pleasures is to gather the fresh eggs from the chicken coop just before lunchtime to make a "Hunger Gap Omelet" with winter garden greens. Begin by making an basic omelet recipe. I'm partial to Julia Child's recipe in *Mastering the Art of French Cooking*. To fill the omelet, add:

- ½ cup chopped fresh kale
- ⅛ cup (approx.) Parmesan cheese
- ⅛ cup (approx.) grated winter carrots fresh from the garden
- ⅛ cup (approx.) garden beans from the freezer, semi-thawed
- ⅛ cup (approx.) chopped homegrown onion

MY GREAT-GRANDMOTHER'S RECIPES

Forgotten recipes recorded by my great-grandmother, Lexia Dastrup Warnock, 1890–1985, in Sigurd, Utah. While not always recipes that we would use today, these recipes are a culinary time capsule. In one case, she recorded in the same recipe both the traditional and more modern way to can garden vegetables.

Butter Soup

Cut into chunks potatoes, carrots, and onions. Cook in water until tender. Salt and pepper to taste, and add a couple of tablespoons of butter before serving.

Wall Cleaner

(apparently some kind of dough ball used to erase wall marks)

- 1 cup flour
- ½ cup cold water
- 2 Tbsp. ammonia
- 1 Tbsp. coal oil
- 2 Tbsp. salt

Mix to a paste and boil, stirring until dough can be handled.

Lazy Housewife Pickles

- 1 cup salt
- 1 cup sugar
- ½ cup dry mustard
- 1 quart water
- 3 quarts vinegar

Fill jars with cucumbers. Then pour mix on cold. Seal with glass top lids if possible. Makes 10 quarts.

Omit mustard and add dill weed for dill pickles. Omit mustard for mixed pickles when using cauliflower, onions, and string beans.

Pickled Beets

Juice:

- 1 cup sugar,
- 2 cups beet juice
- 2 cups vinegar

Cook beets until done. Cut and put into bottles. Pour boiling juice over beets and seal. Can be spiced with cloves and allspice. New method: pack cold, put on lids, and process in water bath.

Pickled Green Beans

Blanch beans 4 minutes.

Pack in jars, with dill and garlic to suit your taste, usually 1 garlic clove and a spring of dill to each pint jar. Bring to a boil:

- 2 cups vinegar
- 2 cups water
- ¼ cup salt
- ¼ tsp. cayenne pepper (scant)

Pour over beans and seal. Process 10 minutes to cook beans.

Canker medicine

- 1 tsp. each of Goldenseal, bayberries, nutmeg, copperas, alum, borax
- 1 lb honey
- 1 pint strong sage tea

Burn copperas until brown, then add all to the sage tea and boil down to about half.

Root Beer

My grandma recalled in her memoirs making root beer as a child using dandelion roots and other roots from the yard and garden. She couldn't remember what roots.

Mixture:

- 2 cups sugar
- 1 level tsp. yeast
- ⅕ bottle of root beer extract per gallon
- Add warm (not hot) water

Seal. Lay on side in a warm place for 24 hours. Chill to serve

BIBLIOGRAPHY

"About Us." Seedsavers.org. Accessed 8/3/2010.

Alterman, Tabitha. "More Great News About Free Range Eggs." *Mother Earth News,* February/March 2009.

American Livestock Breeds Conservancy. "Rare Breed Facts—Why Raise Rare Breeds?" http://albc-usa.org/EducationalResources/rarebreedfacts.html. Accessed 8/3/10.

Ashworth, Suzanne. *Seed to Seed: Seed Saving and Growing Techniques for Vegetable Gardeners.* Seed Savers Exchange, 2002, 41, 49, 54, 88, 136, 137.

Bancroft, Hubert Howe. *History of Utah, 1540–1886.* San Francisco: The History Company, 1889.

"Bill of Particulars (1845)." *Nauvoo Neighbor.* October 29, 1845, as cited in B.H. Roberts, *A Comprehensive History of the Church of Jesus Christ of Latter-day Saints,* 1:539–40.

Bubel, Mike and Nancy. *Root Cellaring: Natural Cold Storage of Fruits and Vegetables.* Storey Publishing, 1991.

Burros, Marion. "Poultry Industry Quietly Cuts Back On Antibiotic Use." *New York Times.* Feb. 10, 2002. Accessed at NYTimes.com, 8/3/10.

Carter, Kate B. "Kartchner, Wiliam Decatur." *Our Pioneer Heritage.* International Society, Daughters of the Utah Pioneers. As quoted in "Heritage Gateways" http://heritage.uen.org/companies/Wc19bfa4d6d0c7.htm

"Catalog 2010." Baker Creek Heirloom Seeds.

Center for Biodiversity and Conservation. "Biodiversity and Your Food: Did You Know?" American Museum of Natural History. http://cbc.amnh.org/living/food/index.html. Accessed 8/3/10.

Damerow, Gail. *Storey's Guide to Raising Chickens.* Storey Publishing, 1995.

Farmer, Fannie Merritt. *The Boston Cooking-school Cook Book.* Little and Brown, 1918. Accessed via Bartleby.com.

Gorman, Christine; David Bjerklie, and Alice Park. "Playing Chicken with Our Antibiotics." *TIME* magazine. 21 Jan. 2002. Accessed at Time.com, 8/3/10.

Graves, Will. *Raising Poultry Successfully.* Williamson Publishing, 1985.

History of Brigham Young (1847) p. 103–4. Accessed at LDS.org.

Journal of John Alma Vance. Facsimile. In possession of author.

"Lindon Family's Large, Green Egg May Be Record Setter." *Daily Herald*, Jan. 14, 2010. Accessed via HeraldExtra.com, 8/3/10.

"Lesson 41: The Saints Settle the Salt Lake Valley" Primary 5: Doctrine and Covenants: Church History (1997) p. 238. Accessed via lds.org 8/3/10.

"Making a Healthful Use of Stored Wheat." LDShealth.ning.com. Accessed 8/3/2010.

Our Sixty Years: Memoirs of Irvin and Lexia Warnock. Family publication in possession of author (1971).

Petrini, Carlo. *Slow Food Nation: Why Our Food Should be Good, Clean, and Fair.* Rezzoli Ex Librs, 2007.

Rossier, Jay. *Living With Chickens.* David & Charles, 2005.

Seymour, John Seymour. *The Self-sufficient Life and How to Live It.* DK Publishing, 2009.

Shinkle, Peter. "Monsato Sends Seed-Saving Farmer to Prison." *St. Louis Post-Dispatch.* May 7, 2003. http://www.organicconsumers.org/ge/prison051403.cfm. Accessed via Organic Consumers Association 8/3/2010.

True and Faithful: A Tribute to Lexia Dastrup Warnock, 1890-1985. Family compilation in possession of author (2009).

Ussery, Harvey. "Working With Broody Hens: Let Mama Do It." *Backyard Poultry Magazine*, June/July 2006.

Warnock, Caleb. "Preserve Your Experience and Heritage in a Poultry Journal." *Backyard Poultry,* Feb/March 2009.

———. "Rethinking Perennials: Flowers are Going to Rise." *13th Annual Hidden Garden Tour Guidebook,* 2008.

Watson, Bruce. "The Lowly Dandelion." *Yankee.* Mar. 2001, vol. 65 issue 2, p. 78. Accessed through Academic Search Premier 8/3/10.

Whitney, Orson Ferguson. "Anson Call." *History of Utah: Biographical* (1904). Accessed via Google Books 8/3/10.

———. "Dimick Baker Huntington" *History of Utah: Biographical* (1904). Accessed via Google Books 8/3/10.

———. "Julian Moses" *History of Utah: Biographical* (1904). Accessed via Google Books 8/3/10.

———. "Lorenzo Dow Young." *History of Utah: Biographical* (1904). Accessed via Google Books 8/3/10.

"William Clayton Journal, July 22, 1847" LDS Church Archives, as quoted in "Mormon Pioneer Trail History" Utah.com.

INDEX

ABOUT THE AUTHOR

Caleb Warnock was raised in the kitchens and gardens of the last generation to provide family meals without relying on the grocery store. He has won more than a dozen awards for journalism and literature, including the Utah Arts Council Original Writing Contest and the David O. McKay Essay Contest. His writing ranges from articles on wolf-watching in Yellowstone to backyard poultry-keeping to perennial gardening. He has taught writing for the past decade.

Caleb teaches "Forgotten Skills" classes ranging from winter gardening, pioneer jams and jellies, growing early and long-keeper vegetable, raising chickens, and much more. To reach the author, visit CalebWarnock.blogspot.com or calebwarnock@yahoo.com.